WHERE KINDNESS SPOKE

Best practices of a lieutenant governor...
through her Leadership Nuggets, Tweets, Blogs and Photos

WHERE KINDNESS SPOKE
Best practices of a lieutenant governor...
through her Leadership Nuggets, Tweets, Blogs and Photos

Shivani Arora

STERLING

STERLING PUBLISHERS (P) LTD.
Regd. Office: A1/256 Safdarjung Enclave,
New Delhi-110029. Cin: U22110DL1964PTC211907
Phone: +91 82877 98380
e-mail: mail@sterlingpublishers.in
www.sterlingpublishers.in

WHERE KINDNESS SPOKE
Best practices of a Lieutenant Governor
through her Leadership Nuggets, Tweets, Blogs and Photos
© 2020, Shivani Arora
ISBN 978-81-944007-1-4

All rights are reserved.
No part of this publication may be reproduced, stored in a retrieval system or transmitted, in any form or by any means, mechanical, photocopying, recording or otherwise, without prior written permission of the original publisher.

Printed in India

Printed and Published by Sterling Publishers Pvt. Ltd.,
Plot No. 13, Ecotech-III, Greater Noida - 201306,
Uttar Pradesh, India

FOREWORD

School history and civics textbooks have referred to governors as ceremonial figureheads. Many holders of the gubernatorial office have been accused of being pliable agents of the Centre, the record of some outstanding governors, especially down South, who lent dignity to the Raj Bhavan, notwithstanding.

Little would Shivani Arora have imagined during her teens when she first developed a fascination for the dynamic IPS officer Dr Kiran Bedi, that her fan-girl phase would undergo a metamorphosis of sorts. From sending adulatory letters to her role model, then the Inspector General of Tihar Jail and a Magsaysay awardee, to closely interacting with Dr Bedi in her present avatar as the Lt Governor of Puducherry, life has come full circle.

If the late Dr Abdul Kalam shattered the palace intrigue of Rashtrapati Bhavan with his outreach initiatives as the People's President, Dr Bedi has transformed the functioning and perception of Raj Nivas in Puducherry. The Lt Governor's people-centric approach, reflected in surprise inspections at government offices or regular public interface, all captured on video, which have gone viral on the social media, has undoubtedly caught the fancy of the author, even as it has been resented by the elected government that views Dr Bedi's style as a violation of the Constitutional line of control.

Where Kindness Spoke lucidly documents the unconventional style of a Lt Governor with a distinct "insider outside" ring. While Shivani veers close to a hagiography, her journalism background helps her infuse a semblance of objectivity, in terms of telling the story like it is.

With an overkill of negativity in the media today, coupled with cynicism and disenchantment in the minds of citizens with respect to public functionaries, Lt Governor Bedi is like a breath of fresh air. Far from being the proverbial rubber-stamp, she has brought energy and an infectious passion for change to her office. How many citizens today queue up for selfies with Lt Governors? Or how many children get to sit on a Lt Governor's chair? This chronicle of Shivani Arora is reason enough to re-visit the uncharitable reference to Lt Governors in those school text books!

The book's tag line could easily be – the audacity of hope.

SANJAY PINTO

Advocate, Madras High Court
Columnist, Author, Political Analyst
Former Resident Editor, NDTV 24X7

PREFACE

> **LEADERSHIP NUGGET**
>
> A leader does not work for others, he works for himself. He chooses to serve. A leader is self-driven. He doesn't need to be told, he tells himself. He does not do a job. He creates service for himself and others. He has a higher purpose to serve and he spreads joy at work.
>
> — Kiran Bedi

I distinctly remember the afternoon of 22 May 2016 when the news on television flashed – Dr Kiran Bedi appointed LG of Puducherry. As much as I was delighted that Kiranji, who had been my inspiration since childhood, was going to occupy such an important constitutional post, I had butterflies in my stomach. Butterflies because I had just received a confirmation from her to be at my college for an important event in September – and now this posting! I wondered what would happen. Will she still honour the invitation? I sent her a congratulatory message and reminded her about the invitation. She replied saying, "Will keep up my commitment with you."

This was my first personal interaction with Kiranji or "Ma'am" as I refer to her now. I have been in awe of her work as LG and have been fortunate to be a part of her creative team and even work with her closely. She calls me her "K-pedia" and I call her my forever inspiration and my godmother.

True to her leadership style, she redefined the role of the LG. She defined her purpose of being there to be on a mission to serve people and make Puducherry a "Prosperous Puducherry". She has remained self-driven and has carved a special place for herself in the constitutional history of our country as an LG who refused to be a rubber stamp, but one who opened the gates of Rajnivas to the common people and served them with utmost love and affection. Her kindness spoke through her work and won the hearts of the people.

When it comes to kindness as a leadership trait, some people believe that this could be a weakness. But actually kindness strengthens leadership. Some traits which exhibit kindness in leadership include being generous in giving and receiving, being caring and responsive to people's needs, communicating with a personal touch, valuing views of others while giving constructive feedback, counselling and mentoring and accommodating personal views. Each of these traits have been the highlight of Dr Kiran Bedi's leadership style. Hence the title of this book.

The first part of this book is an attempt at briefly describing her work as LG in the last three years, how I observed it both as an outsider and as part of her team and how I connected it with her tweets, blogs and leadership nuggets – all of them were the expressions of her thoughts.

The second part of the book gives a deeper insight on how she brought about a new model of governance based on teamwork, transparency and field work, which not just governments but also corporates and other organizations can adopt to make a difference to their way of functioning.

Contents

PART - A

1. When Top Cop Became The LG — 3
2. The Initial Days — 5
3. Leadership With A Difference — 7
4. Self-Learning And Mentoring — 12
5. Taking The Bull-By-The-Horns — 16
6. The Tussle For Power — 19
7. Water Rich Puducherry — 24
8. Ensuring Financial Prudence — 28
9. Value For Time And Team Work — 32
10. Following The Rule Of Law: A Murder Of Democracy — 36
11. The Issue Of Nominated Mlas — 36
12. The Historic Dharna — 38
13. Dr Kiran Bedi's Views On Hard Work — 41
14. A True Visionary Leader — 42

PART - B

15. The Inspirational Connect — 46
16. Best Practices — 49

17.	Teaming Up People As A Think Thank	51
18.	Forming Team Rajnivas And The 10 Am Meeting	51
19.	Ushering In An Era Of Openness:	57
20.	Making Rajnivas A People Nivas	57
21.	A Beacon Of Hope: Open House	58
22.	Where Dreams Come True Visitors Hour	64
23.	Inspiring Through Films: Rajnivas Film Series	67
24.	Engaging Great Minds: Rajnivas Lecture Series	70
25.	When Officers Became Teachers: Rajnivas Leadership Series	72
26.	Appreciating Art And Culture Rajnivas Art And Culture Series	75
27.	A Feeling Of Togetherness: Celebrating Festivals	77
28.	Building Future Leaders Interns For Social Leadership – Rajnivas Youth Engagement Programme	79
29.	Moving Out Of The Comfort Zone: Weekend Morning Rounds	83
30.	Mentoring, Self-Evaluation And Appraisals	89
31.	One-On-One Meetings	90
32.	Field Visits To Departments	92
33.	Self-Evaluation Tests: Weekly And Monthly Reviews	99
34.	Surprise/Incognito Visits	103
35.	The Use Of Communication And Technology	108
36.	The Creative Team And Documentation	109
37.	Prosperous Puducherry Whatsapp Group	112

38.	Declaration Of Weekly Disposal Of Files	114
39.	Monthly Message To Citizens	118
40.	Networking And Collaborations	122
41.	The Rajnivas Outreach Program	123
42.	Co Opting Human Resources	127
43.	Awards And Recognition: A Trip That Was A True Revelation	133
44.	A Perfect Model Of Leadership And Governance	138
45.	Gratitude	141
46.	About The Author	143

PART - A

⟶ WHEN TOP COP BECAME THE LG

> **LEADERSHIP NUGGET**
> Leadership is freedom to be fully responsible, fully accountable. Full accounting of one's own actions, omissions and commissions.
>
> — Kiran Bedi

When Dr Kiran Bedi took over as the LG of Puducherry, from the beginning itself she walked a path that no one had taken earlier. She defined her own purpose and her own style of working as LG. One of her first steps was to address a gathering of officers and guests after taking oath as LG. This was not a regular practice but she had come prepared with her mission of making Puducherry a "Prosperous Puducherry" and she even had a mantra ready to give to her team here. Her mantra was TEA –trust, empowerment and accountability.

> **AN EXCERPT FROM HER OATH SPEECH**
> And for me today, this new responsibility is a form of worship…to serve the most beautiful part of India. I am here to give it all I have.

We all visualize a #Prosperous Puducherry and we shall deliver this responsibility through the three principle mantras. The first one being Trust. This would mean working with integrity in all forms – financial, administrative and intention.

The second mantra is Empowerment. This means enabling and enhancing optimum utilization of resources while addressing concerns. It also means promoting and reliance through training, mentoring and more.

The third and the final mantra is Accountability. Not just to the people but also to yourself. It means implementing and promoting respect for the law.

Together these mantras form the acronym TEA.

She swung into action from the very first day. During the initial days, some of the practices she started, which were based on kindness, set the tone for the work pattern she adopted subsequently and follows till now.

THE INITIAL DAYS

> @TheKiranBedi: Thank u God for enabling me a position where I can do & get things done in a collective manner as I always imagined
>
> 1 July 2016

Within days of taking over as LG, Dr Kiran Bedi brought in so many changes that the people in Puducherry were in awe of this new leader who had just come in and was already reaching out to them to help them. In the first week itself she started the system of open house and the gates of Rajnivas were thrown open to public who had grievances and 40 tokens were issued every day. This was a practice Dr Bedi had started in New Delhi when she was special advisor to the LG of Delhi, Tejinder Khanna. It was started here in Puducherry and continues to be practised till date. Another step she took was to ban the use of sirens. "I was driving around the city and was ashamed to see the siren being blown and people moving aside out of fear. People's right to freedom of movement should not be hindered due to these sirens," she said. Tree planting drives were planned and every government office in Puducherry swung into action. For the first time officers started to reach office at 9 a.m. and made themselves available to help people. Dr Bedi started to live and make use of each day to the fullest just like she had read in her father's diary when she was packing her bags to come to Puducherry.

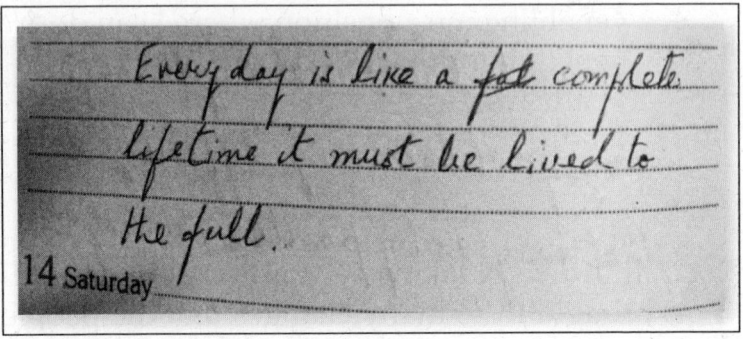

All these practices, which she started within the first fortnight of assuming charge, were driven by the urge to be a kind leader who was there to serve people through her position. This what made it truly a leadership with a difference.

⇀ LEADERSHIP WITH A DIFFERENCE

> **LEADERSHIP NUGGET**
>
> **F O G**
>
> **F:** Finding time to meet/visit the spot or field of one needing a solution and engaging with people on the site.
>
> **O:** Opening up your office for a fixed time/day for anyone to see you – Open House
>
> **G:** Gifts. We as leaders receive several gifts because of our official position. It is for us to decide which are from our loved ones and which ones are because of the position we hold. Ones which are because of position are to be kept aside to be given away to the ones who need them more. This is when your integrity quotient will come into play for your own self. Watch it.
>
> — Kiran Bedi

Dr Kiran Bedi redefined the role of the LG and people saw a sea-change in governance. True to the above nugget she has followed all the three FOG.

Finding Time to Meet: She made time to go out in the field and attend to issues. Mornings during weekends were dedicated to rounds with the team where she went to the problem and attended to it. "Language is a huge barrier for me so I decided that if people can't listen to me they can at least see me. I therefore started stepping out every weekend early morning with my team so people could see their LG and I could go the problem and sort it out for them," says Dr Bedi. She has done more than 200 weekend rounds and from reviving lakes, to cleaning garbage dumps and even making Puducherry water-rich, these weekend rounds have been absolute game changers.

An excerpt from her blog on weekend rounds

What is weekend morning round and why
———————————————

Today is 201 weekend morning round
****

This means as "Team Rajnivas" we have done 201 weekend rounds in 100 weeks.

(Saturdays and Sundays 6.30 a.m.)

I took charge as Lt Governor on 29 May 2016. I started my weekend morning rounds from the very first weekend of my responsibility here as Lt Governor.

My first round came as a response to Hon'ble Speaker's grievance from his constituency about choked water drains. And he bringing in the residents' delegation to visit me.

They wanted a solution.

On their request I went to the residential colony and saw it in need of strong intervention.

The second request for a field visit came from MLA Mr Laxmi Narayan for Grand Canal cleaning. I went with him too and saw for myself the situation pretty bad then. The Grand Canal used to stink heavily.

Seeing and witnessing both the places I realised the need for direct visits rather than waiting for paper reports as solutions to these required close coordination amongst Dept.

Reality on ground too may be quite different. I felt that to improve things faster I will have to step out of comfort zone and do regular field visits.

I chose weekend mornings because it's my own time and pace. Office work does not have to wait.

So I chose 6 a.m./ 6.30 a.m. To start the day. As I am an early riser by habit.

Team Rajnivas was formed.

Open Up the Office: Under Dr Bedi's leadership, Rajnivas has become a people's nivas, a lok nivas and now even a vishwasnivas. From having a fixed time for open house and listening to grievances to starting a visitors' hour where people get to look around the historic Rajnivas and also interact with Her Excellency and celebrating all festivals with the people of Puducherry, Rajnvas has been open to the public for the very first time in the history of Puducherry.

Gifts: At Rajnivas she receives a lot of gifts every day but all of these gifts go into the Rajnivas gift cupboard and they are given away to people – to swachchata workers, to officers and of course to children. The shawls she receives are given to swachchata workers. It is very touching to see Ma'am cycling around the city, stopping by these workers and thanking them for keeping the city clean and giving them these shawls. All other gifts, be it curios, books, fruits, shawls, stationery, are all given away. "These gifts are not coming to Kiran Bedi, they are coming to the LG and they belong to this office. I take nothing from here. We instead give it back to the people who deserve them," says Dr Bedi.

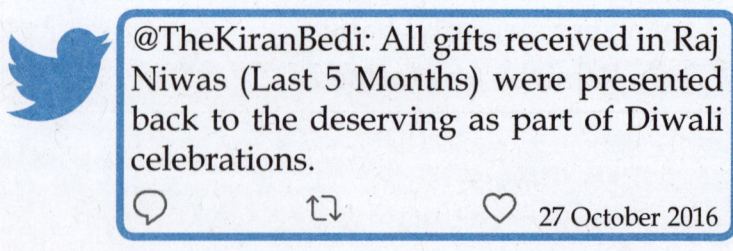

@TheKiranBedi: All gifts received in Raj Niwas (Last 5 Months) were presented back to the deserving as part of Diwali celebrations.

27 October 2016

> **Sacred**space
>
> *Bearing Gifts*
>
> You bear gifts and lights – not for yourself, but for others. Remember that all the gifts you are carrying in your life are for others. Anyone who comes to you, offer them your gifts.
>
> **Sri Sri Ravi Shankar**

Dr Bedi reached out to the people in the kindest way she could through open house, weekend rounds and sharing gifts. The leader within her also wanted to reach out to the officers and use her expertise to help them work better. So she began meeting them, visiting offices and having review meetings.

SELF-LEARNING AND MENTORING

> **LEADERSHIP NUGGET**
>
> A leader accomplishes a piece of work with such skill that nothing else is left to be done. This is real proficiency. For that to happen he remains focussed and also continues to update his skills through constant learning. Which is why self-training and training of team members is crucial.
>
> —Kiran Bedi

For Dr Bedi, her work as LG does not restrict her to just signing files or occupying the ceremonial position. She believes she is here to bring a change in Puducherry and constantly likes to learn and upgrade her knowledge. She also believes in mentoring and helping people self-evaluate. This is what leads to one-on-one interactions with officers and secretaries, visits to departments, self-evaluation examinations and so on. Each of her one-on-one's were eye-openers for officers and some even wished they had been given such mentoring at the beginning of their career. Her visits to departments revealed that officers lacked knowledge about their own work and that there was space for improvement. The lessons she gave them were precious management lessons and their self-evaluation exams actually made them read up and improve their knowledge and even do SWOT analysis.

@TheKiranBedi: Start of the day daily at 9.30 AM with a One on One with one Secretary. Today was with Secretary IT. It really helps. It updates and helps the officer gain more focus on planning for the month, focus, training and more.

27 October 2016

BLOG ON PERFORMANCE APPRAISAL

What does it take to self earn an "outstanding" or even a "very good" annual appraisal.
Here are my observations.
* * * * * * * * * * * * * * * *

Here is my "guidance" for you to earn an outstanding appraisal during the remaining period of the assessment period. (I have no doubt this is your aspiration).

Here are some generic ones applicable to all. Every Dept has specifics too which you can and should be identified by you as the leader and shall be assessed by me as your reviewing or accepting authority, at the time of assessment.

1. Frequent Field visits with stake holders to understand their problems time-to-time.

With a planned calendar. Also cover all sections of your beneficiaries.

2. Engage yourself directly in your unit visits to connect with, cutting ranks.

   See and feel the place. Is it using technology to the maximum it can to improve data entry and analysis?

3. Be a resource provider and a guide. Banking on who and what you have and not wait and wish for what is not and wait for that to happen. Time will not wait for any of us.

4. Plan and propose improvements and follow them up to see if these got implemented. Which means you must maintain minutes of the visit and the guidance given. Use them for recall and assessment. Track your files/proposals.

5. It's also a mentoring visit where you take the Dept performance to the next level by mandating self-study, team training and then you go and take a test.

6. Maintain a planned schedule for yourself and ensure your unit heads also do so. Plan your review meeting. While keeping the door open for other eventualities.

7. Once a month at least bring all your units together to communicate and share collective performance and priorities of the month and any specific unit.

8. Review that first before you go to add new ones. Volunteer coordination. Speak and connect with peers to expedite decisions.
9. Be firm on financial prudence and application of rules and procedures. Deviation only be on justified and not on external obligations or acceptance. Track your important files. Do not lose sight of them. Your responsibility is not just to pass the file but in their implementation.
10. Promote strict adherence to rule of law and financial prudence and transparency in all appointments and decisions.
11. Respect guidance. And provide the feedback of action taken on it from time-to-time. And come back for clarifications if needed. Respond to queries. Do not take your seniors for granted. They too have a tracker.
12. I Shall continue to guide you as it is my duty to do so.
13. Please use this if you find it worthwhile. It shall stand you in good stead in your career.

Amid all her work, when she listened to grievances in the open house, a complaint that came to her repeatedly was regarding medical admissions and how meritorious students were not being given seats because they were not able to the afford the capitation fees asked. Hence she stepped in to take the bull-by-the-horns and help the students not just as a leader but as a kind mother.

TAKING THE BULL-BY-THE-HORNS

> **LEADERSHIP NUGGET**
>
> Leaders begin with what is urgent but alongside kickstart change in areas which cannot wait but need some time. They do not wait. They make things happen. They perform to transform.
>
> — Kiran Bedi

Dr Bedi, during the last three years as LG, has worked on several issues simultaneously. One issue which she took up on an urgent basis was that of the medical admissions. Who will forget how she walked into the CENTAC (Centralised Admission Committee)office, questioned the officers there and put her own job at stake to fight for the students. From asking for a CBI enquiry to taking the case up to the Supreme Court, she fought all the way to get justice for the students. She met stiff opposition from the political fraternity but nothing deterred her from fighting for the students who were deserving but were being fleeced. seats.

Medical admissions in India are a huge business as there is always an option of "buying a seat" rather than getting a seat allotted by the CENTAC. The prevalence of this practice has led several families into penury while lining the pockets of the seat sellers.

@TheKiranBedi: #CBI today demolished an historical complex of corruption in medical seats in Puducherry which people had reconciled to. No more. Thanku CBI

@TheKiranBedi: #Medical seats scam in Puducherry is a case of criminal culpability & administrative failure at political and administrative levels @PMOIndia

20 September 2017

AN EXCERPT FROM HER MICROBLOG ON THE HISTORIC SC ORDER

The Rajnivas secretariat intervened last year when no one in our political and departmental administration in Puducherry was willing to protect the interest of hapless but aspirational students. It's an even tin history of the UT when Rajnivas had to stand up by itself. Needy students and their parents were seen running from pillar to post. The open house at Rajnivas brought forth the evidence of apathy. This is when Team Rajnivas stepped in to take the bull-by-the-horns. It faced a huge hostile backlash (media reports of that period are replete of this). The Rajnivas secretariat brought in GOI in the accountability right upto the PMO. Meanwhile, these efforts led to the stepping in of a missionary and well places lawyer in Chennai, Mr V.B.R. Menon who took up this cause probono. All this was closely observed by the chief bench of the Madras High Court and commented upon. An interim judicial order led to capping of the fees charged by the Deemed Medical Universities and need for a committee to fix their fees. We were defended by our ASGs at minimum cost while the medical mafia was represented by a battery of expensive lawyers. The powerful lobby took the matter to SC for a stay against the order of the HC, using its money and muscle clout. They have failed. Justice has won. The SC order not just does justice to Puducherry but to all other states, if they choose to apply. This order is a final nail in the coffin of the historical exploitation by a nexus which existed in exploiting the meritorious poor for decades not only in Puducherry but around the country.

Even as she looked into the various issues that the union territory was grappling with and attending to them, the issue of the powers of LG came up. At every juncture she met with opposition, challenging her powers as LG.

THE TUSSLE FOR POWER

> **LEADERSHIP NUGGET**
>
> For a leader doing the right thing in the right way never goes out of style. A true leader remains steadfast on principles and is uncompromising on fundamentals. He never compromises on integrity or commits a breach of trust towards the responsibility he entrusts himself with.
>
> — Kiran Bedi

Ever since she took over as LG of Puducherry Dr Bedi has been loggerheads with the CM. The reason is that she refuses to be a mere ceremonial head or a rubber stamp. On the contrary, she goes by the rule-book and always believes in doing the right thing at the right time. This tussle with the CM has been long drawn. He initially spoke through his chief secretary, then through a minister and finally began to speak himself. Dr Bedi has been known for her integrity, honesty and righteousness and when she is LG there is absolutely no space for corruption. This has been a huge point of conflict between her and the CM. She has taken on one issue after another patiently and dealt with it.

When it came to the Chief secretary, she had the CS replaced by the Central Government and managed to bring in some harmony in the working of the government.

AN EXCERPT FROM HER BLOG ON THE ROLE OF THE CHIEF SECRETARY

CS PIVOT OF PEACE AND HARMONY

Experience reveals that the role of the CS is the most vital in the peace and progress of any state. He or she can steer all round development based on missionary zeal and focus. His honest notings or advise on the file and in meetings, based on facts of the case, rules of business, financial rules, administrative rules or policy matters, is the foundation for all right decisions by the Government.

He is not a post-office but a key driver of the change and protector and guarantor of integrity. He is the "Aadhar". He unites and is a mentor. He is also the last office in the bureaucracy for access by people with any grievance. It is this which needs to be appreciated. The primary reason for this not being fully realized in certain cases is perhaps " sense of insecurity" coming through appraisal, performance reports and anxiety over the next position.

If primary focus is personal survival, then the State is bound to merely limp and progress only in parts and suffer in many. There will be discord, scams and complaints. One right person at this key position with right intention with devotion and zeal is the key to overall development. Even if the CS is overruled by powers that be, he is the senior most professional advisor.

He is accountable. He cannot say he did not know. He must have his systems of management to know how to correct anything. He can intervene in anything as all departments report to him.

Remember once he records correctly, no power will be able to overrule him on merits of the case without putting themselves at risk as the file always speaks.

Hence the CS of any State or UT is the pivot of peace, harmony and order. Of course, there can be instances of honest differences of opinion. But then each one is responsible for the recorded decisions they take. They have to be justifiable. The advice of the CS therefore must be professional and honest, without fear or favour.

When it came to the CM, she pulled out the rule-book and listed out the powers she ha as LG because Puducherry is a Union Territory. This issue has been challenged in court and remains an issue till date but Dr Bedi insists on working according to the rule-book.

AN EXCERPT FROM HER BLOG ON POWERS OF LG

WHO TELLS HON. CM WHAT LAID-DOWN RESPONSIBILITIES OF A LT GOVERNOR ARE?

So what does the Honourable CM (V Narayanasamy) want? A rubber stamp or a responsible administrator? This is the real question.

The CM, according to the news, desires an endorser. One who may let wrongs happen even when people are suffering injustice. Wants an LG who clears files without seeking clarity. One who appoints people as per demands of vested interests. One who releases money even if it's not budgeted for. Hence borrow and spend. One who promotes officers even when there are either no posts or poor performance or no reason.

One who should do nothing and see nothing and say nothing. Just be an onlooker. And pass time, enjoy benefits of an expensive establishment called Rajnivas. Stay isolated. Do not meet people. Do not question officers. Do not interfere. Just do as he tells, even in writing. I have received several such letters from him).

Most of all, the CM wants me to get lots of money from the Government of India, even when they can't spend well what they have. Even when revenue generating tourism is loss-making. This is called wishful thinking. In reality he can feel empowered and enthused that there is someone here to help him clean up the mess in his Puducherry. It's mine only now by adoption, it is his by birth. It's a question of what the CM wants. That is the real issue.

What does a CM want and what does an LG want? Both have their responsibilities laid down in the UT act and in the business rules. It is how he reads or misreads. Or ignores reading. Or does not want to face the realities of the situation today.

People are crying for justice. Rajnivas is becoming their last hope. As per open house, Puducherry needs justice, integrity and good governance. How will they get it? Who will give it to them? Who will speak up for them? Not an onlooker but someone whose heart is for them. Someone who serves them with a sense of selflessness. One who places people before positions.

Water is the basic necessity for life and the best a leader can do is to work towards ensuring that there is sufficient water for the people. It is with this thought Dr Bedi took up the challenge of making Puducherry "water rich".

WATER RICH PUDUCHERRY

> **LEADERSHIP NUGGET**
>
> "I alone cannot change the world but I can cast a stone across the water to create many ripples," said Mother Teresa. Leadership creates ripples to set the change in motion the moment it is convinced that a change is essential and status quo is not serving the purpose. It then takes a risk and begins causing the ripples. It does not lose time but captures it at the earliest opportunity it can and casts the first stone to set in motion the churning.
>
> — Kiran Bedi

During one of her early weekend rounds to temple ponds, Dr Bedi said, "If there is a legacy I will leave behind for Puducherry it will be that of water." As she went around to lakes, ponds and villages she realized Puducherry was starving for water. A visit to water channels opened her eyes to the harsh reality that these channels were full of thick vegetation and needed to be desilted before the monsoons. The PWD did not have sufficient budget and so Dr Bedi brought in the community to help, just the way she had used community help to reform Tihar Jail. CSR (Corporate Social Responsibility) support poured in and many urban and rural channels were desilted. During the monsoons neither did the city get flooded nor were the villages inundated. On the contrary, they managed to get water to use for agriculture. She actually brought back the historic model of community participation and has put Puducherry on the path to becoming water-rich which will surely have a ripple effect and encourage future leaders and the community to take forward the legacy she has bestowed.

@TheKiranBedi:

To make #PuducherryWaterRich we r seeking a collaborative model for desilting tanks, canals & ponds. Dept Concerned shall connect the donor with the contractor providing JCP machinery. Donor to pay provider directly. It's a win win model for all. Call 1031 for the offer ASAP

♡ 24 September 2018

EXCERPT OF HER BLOG ON WATER RICH PUDUCHERRY

It is the duty of every public official to change things for the better where it is required to be done. As this is the reason for being given administrative responsibilities. He or she fails as an official if he does not provide solutions.

For instance, when we had no funds in the government budget to clean 86 km of our water channels and the monsoon was around the corner and our lakes and tanks were empty, and water table dipping, what should responsible public officials do?

Give up and leave them as they are or look or solutions and options? We looked for solutions. We appealed on social media and people responded in abundance. Because they too want to see water-rich Puducherry. As public officials we must make choices every day. Regardless of the hostility the change may bring.

Change for a public servant is not for themselves but for larger good. Today this is being achieved. Thanks to our combined efforts, community support and with a good monsoon, Puducherry will have sufficient water for agriculture, industry, sanitation and domestic use for years to come. Even those telling white lies will also benefit

The purpose is met.

But this met opposition, too. Her office was blamed for misusing funds but she made it very clear that Rajnivas had worked only as a facilitator and that the donor was directly paying the contractor. With her persistent efforts today, Puducherry has beautifully desilted water channels.

@TheKiranBedi: "Ignorance is always afraid of change" JL Nehru

14 October 2018

> Friends,
>
> From the published statements of Honourable CM today, he appears very happy to see "his own" Puducherry become water-rich, despite his inadequacy to provide funds to clear age old 83 km of unattended severely choked with thick vegetation water channels filling major lakes, 84 tanks and 600 ponds by the end of the NE monsoon this year.
>
> The HCM instead of being grateful to the sponsors for extending material support in the form of machinery and payments directly to contractors, is trying to pick holes which do not exist.

Her gesture to make Puducherry water rich has been filled with utmost kindness. Whether she worked on desilting water channels or dealt with issues of freebies during festivals, her financial powers were always questioned but she remained firm in ensuring financial prudence.

27

⇌ ENSURING FINANCIAL PRUDENCE

> **LEADERSHIP NUGGET**
>
> Being a Trusted Leader is a social asset. An Un-Trustworthy leader is a liability on society. A trustworthy leader provides for people. An untrustworthy Leader serves himself first to let people go bankrupt & be dependent.
>
> — Kiran Bedi

Ensuring financial prudence has been one of the greatest challenges that Dr Bedi has faced as LG. "When I agreed to take up this post the only thing the honourable PM told me was to handle the financial situation well and I promised him I would do so," says Dr Bedi and she has truly lived up to that in her three-year tenure. No file that was sent to Rajnivas was signed without checking if budgets were available and she did not concede to demands like freebies for all during Pongal which became a huge point of tussle between her and the CM. Puducherry has been in huge debt and she has been tirelessly working to ensure financial prudence so that borrowings can be reduced. Grants-in-aid is another area where she has faced immense challenges, but she refused to give in, citing rules and the need to ensure financial prudence. She has worked as a trustworthy leader to provide for the people not just for the present, but also for their future.

@TheKiranBedi: Making Grants In Aid truly conditional and performed oriented. This will prevent diversion of limited funds as well as back door irregular recruitments. As well as make for financial accountability. HODs shall certify compliance before release of Grant. #Prosperous Puducherry

25 September 2018

BLOG

Today's news (so far read the English editions, others yet to read)

is having the HCM rant on financial sanctions and policy approvals by the Administrator's office.

The fact is Grants-in-Aid and policy approvals are governed by General Financial Rules and the business rules besides other legal provisions.

And observance of these is the responsibility of the Chief Secretary along with his Secretaries. See Rule 59 of the business Rules. (Chapter VI)

It says as follows.

"The Chief Secretary and the Secretary of the Dept Concerned are several responsible for the careful observance of these rules . . . "

Hence every time the HCM and the Secretariat sends a file to Administrator's office for a sanction and approval, he and they do so because the rules demand it to be sent.

So once a file is received in the LG Secretariat it demands an independent examination by the Administrator.

That is what this approval or sanction implies.

The long prevailing problem lies in the fixed belief of the HCM that the Lt Governor is a mere rubber stamp to endorse whatever is proposed by him.

Then why send the file?

Keep a rubber stamp in your own office and just stamp it yourself.

On one hand HCM sends the file and on the other hand he cries foul and complains when the decision is not in accordance with his wishes.

One cannot send files with a pre-expected decision.

Regrettably, the HCM expects mere endorsements and not independent application of mind, and a decision which suits him even if it is in violation of financial or administrative rules.

This why is the Lt Governor of Puducherry also termed as an Administrator?

I feel sorry for HCM that he continues to expect something which is not legally and morally correct and also what is not in the short and long-term interest of Puducherry.

Dr Bedi is a leader who values every minute of her time and also in the power of teamwork. So she guides her team to make the best of use of every minute optimally and also to work as a team to achieve better results.

VALUE FOR TIME AND TEAM WORK

> **LEADERSHIP NUGGET**
>
> Leaders value their own time and as well as of others. They plan and they execute. They have a reason for every activity they plan or participate in. they have sources of inspiration. They keep no toxic friendships. They generate energy within their time constraints and from the activities they carry out.
>
> — Kiran Bedi

Dr Bedi has been a person who has always valued time and made the best use of every minute of her time. Her day at Rajnivas typically begins with her 10 a.m. meetings. One of the first things she did as soon as she took over was to form the 10 a.m. team or Team Rajnivas, who would meet everyday to plan work, review newspaper clips, grievances and a lot more. From this also evolved the social media team of Rajnivas and till date Dr Kiran Bedi is herself very active in communicating through her WhatsApp groups and all her social media handles remain updated with all activities happening at Rajnivas. The use of social media met stiff opposition as early as January 2017 when

HCM tried to gag the "Prosperous Puducherry" group. But nothing could stop Ma'am from using the power of social networking, which is probably one of her biggest strengths as she is a fantastic communicator and the blogs she sends out on a daily basis stand testimony for this.

> @TheKiranBedi: Prosperous Puducherry WhatsApp groups+of key officers were networking, sharing achievements & redressing public complaints immed. Why gag it?
> 5 January 2017

> @TheKiranBedi: When a leader wants things done he will promote shared info. When he wants control & dependence he will ensure they r kept divided/deprived
> 5 January 2017

SOCIAL MEDIA BLOG FOR NDTV

> One of the first things which struck me after taking over the responsibility as Lieutenant Governor of Puducherry was how do I align all departments serving the people, since government is an organic whole.
>
> Even if each department has a core portfolio, its performance is interrelated with others, and it is also interdependent on others.

In the past, information was shared through postal services. Endorsing copies to each other for information. Hard copies. Some lost on the way. One was not sure when was that message read! Later it became by e-mail, either on one-to-one basis or group mails. What is/was not guaranteed was speed in response.

Remember the challenge before good governance is urgency and the sensitivity of speed. Things changed considerably with a BlackBerry in our hands in the last decade and later by other smartphones. But was the government official a major user? Were government departments major consumers of this new connectivity and smartphones? The general attitude was why create more work? Why put themselves on the block 24x7? I recall the first hand-instrument I received when I reported for my assignment at the UN a decade ago was a BlackBerry along with a mobile phone. Then the two were separate. 3G was not there still.

Fast forward. How much it has all changed. The fastest driver has been the WhatsApp application. This is what I decided to put to maximum use.

Our first endeavour was to bring together all Heads of Departments on one platform to start communicating with each other on a real-time basis and keep up the conversation. Chat with each other. Be friends without even formal dinners.

Once we brought the secretaries and heads together, they brought their own units together on groups. So bigger circle gave birth to inner circles and later to intra-circles of related groups. So we started to become wheels within wheels, somewhere overlapping and connected.

It dramatically improved our information sharing. Meeting notices, minutes of meetings, news clips, photographs, even shared short videos, travels and tour notes, and more. Now there was even a space created for shared achievements missing so far. Most of all ideating.

To ensure that WhatsApp conversation is not lost, we forwarded the content of these groups by e-mail to all. They could then use it for formal file processes on a case-to-case basis. This process has aligned the governance within weeks.

But the biggest breakthrough has come for groups formed for grievance redressal. A message coming on Twitter or Facebook or a text message or an excerpt shared on WhatsApp taken from another source of social networks is getting a response within no time.

The political opposition she continuously faced on all fronts reached its peak when the honourable CM staged a dharna in front of Rajnivas which lasted 6 long days.

FOLLOWING THE RULE OF LAW: A MURDER OF DEMOCRACY
THE ISSUE OF NOMINATED MLAS

> **LEADERSHIP NUGGET**
>
> People always want to see an engaged leadership. Leadership must stand firm in situations where it needs to. With a high energy focus round-the-year and round-the-clock.
>
> — Dr Kiran Bedi

In July 2017 when Dr Kiran Bedi administered oath to three MLAs nominated by the Central Government, little did she know that this matter would become an issue of conflict between her and the elected government in Puducherry. They termed it murder of democracy, they sat on a hunger strike, had a day-long bandh in Puducherry and this matter even went all the way to the Supreme Court. The MLAs were humiliated, not allowed to enter the Assembly, not paid salaries but they remained firm on their stand because they had Dr Bedi's support. She made it very clear that she had gone by the rule-book. And according to the rule-book, she as Lt Governor had the power to administer oath to these MLAs. In December 2018 the Supreme Court ruled in favour of the MLAs and the fact that she had done the right thing by administering oath to them.

@TheKiranBedi: Since when is application of Law a 'murder of democracy'? C d law. Central Govt has d power to Nominate & LG has d power of oath giving..!

6 July 2017

EXCERPT FROM HER BLOG ON NOMINATED MLAS

LAY ASIDE DOUBTS BY KNOWING LAW

Knowing the law removes doubts.

All the three MLAs appointed by the GOI gave the LG office in writing that these authorities concerned to whom they presented the papers with a request for oath were completely evasive and indifferent. Hence, they do not know when and if they would be called upon.

Based on their request and overall assessment of the situation and information also available a considered decision was taken to administer the oath and not leave matters pending which otherwise would have law-and-order implications and cause public disturbance.

THE HISTORIC DHARNA

> **LEADERSHIP NUGGET**
>
> It is a situation which demands a rehearsed response. Leaders to be leaders resolve to fly high against being grounded or being trampled or even being taken for granted.
>
> — Dr Kiran Bedi

On 13 February 2019, even as she worked inside Rajnivas, Dr Bedi was caught unawares when HCM along with his cabinet came and sat on a dharna. Rajnivas was laid siege to and she could not step out even for a personal commitment. HCM demanded reply to a 36-point letter he had earlier sent to LG and refused to budge until his demands were conceded. The next six days saw high intensity drama outside the LG's residence and leaders from across the country coming in to support the dharna, causing so much inconvenience to the public and the staff of Rajnivas. At one point it was even decided to have an open discussion at Gandhi Tidal so public could hear both viewpoints and decide who is right. The dharna went on for six days despite several requests from Dr Bedi and finally ended after a for-hour-long meeting at Rajnivas, discussing all points of the letter.

@TheKiranBedi: Today Raj Nivas was totally surrounded by CM and his agitators. None of us could move out or visitors could come in. Also staff too was blocked from returning to office. An absolutely unlawful situation of law makers turned law breakers. Not sure of tom either.

♡ 13 February 2019

@TheKiranBedi: The Dharna by HCM outside Raj Nivas is over. The HCM, Council Of Ministers, CS and Secretaries, met. It helped clarify and consolidate issues. Am happy Puducherry Government will return to work tom morning. So will the road to Raj Nivas be open for visitors to come to Raj Nivas.

♡ 18 February 2019

EXCERPT OF HER BLOG ON THE HISTORIC DHARNA

MY BLOG OF THE DAY

I welcome the acceptance of the HCM of my suggestion for an open town hall discussion at Gandhi Thidal (venue suggested by HCM) on all points raised in his letter on 7 Feb sent to me. This will enable the general public to hear the views of both sides. The session can be the harbinger of a transparent system of a town hall system which provides grass root democracy and a forum in which status of administration of all departments is known by beneficiaries and the general public on a periodic basis. On matters of finance a town hall by secretary finance can inform people about the budget, the actual financial status of government funds and where utilised. What were the shortages and why and what can be done about it? A town hall of departments with respective ministers will provide the financial status and department policy issues.

The LG office already releases the disposal of files each week. These can now be provided on real time basis. This will go a long way in grievance redressal, feedback as well as check back and forth allegations. Right now it is one-way information.

What better venue than the Gandhi Thidal to promote grass root democracy which empowers people with certified information. If this works Puducherry could offer it as a national model for grass root governance.

Even today she works 18 to 19 hours a day and it is sheer hard work which has brought her this far in her career. Her definition of hard work for public officials is truly worth following.

DR KIRAN BEDI'S VIEWS ON HARD WORK

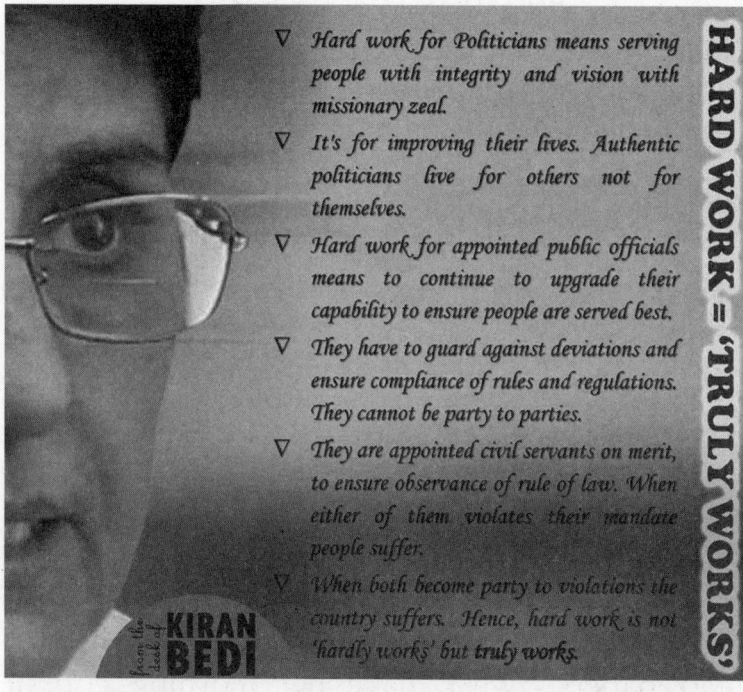

- Hard work for Politicians means serving people with integrity and vision with missionary zeal.
- It's for improving their lives. Authentic politicians live for others not for themselves.
- Hard work for appointed public officials means to continue to upgrade their capability to ensure people are served best.
- They have to guard against deviations and ensure compliance of rules and regulations. They cannot be party to parties.
- They are appointed civil servants on merit, to ensure observance of rule of law. When either of them violates their mandate people suffer.
- When both become party to violations the country suffers. Hence, hard work is not 'hardly works' but truly works.

HARD WORK = 'TRULY WORKS'

from the desk of KIRAN BEDI

All of this makes her a leader like no other but every young girl for whom she is a role-model and inspiration wonders – what does it take to be a Kiran Bedi?

A TRUE VISIONARY LEADER

> **LEADERSHIP NUGGET**
>
> Leaders are news hungry. They look for news, editorials from all sources. Leaders make time for news listening and hence multitask most of the time such as do a gym work out while listening to news. They stay up-to-date.
>
> —Dr Kiran Bedi

As I reflected on this three year tenure of Dr Bedi as LG, the leader she has been and the journey she has traversed from being a super-cop to being a social activist to now holding a constitutional position, I realised what keeps her going is her own desire to work for society. And to keep energised, her morning routine is worth emulating. As I see her work-out on the stepper, read papers, tweet, have her morning cup of chai, all at the same time, I am totally in awe of her energy levels. There are days when she calls out to her team with ideas and the morning hours become the most creative hours of the day. She keeps herself energised throughout the entire day. You can walk into her office at anytime of the day and see her fresh with ideas, ready to work more and more and make a difference to the society and fulfil the purpose for which she is here. But what makes her the person she is? What makes her *the* Kiran Bedi – an epitome of kindness and empathy and a true visionary leader?

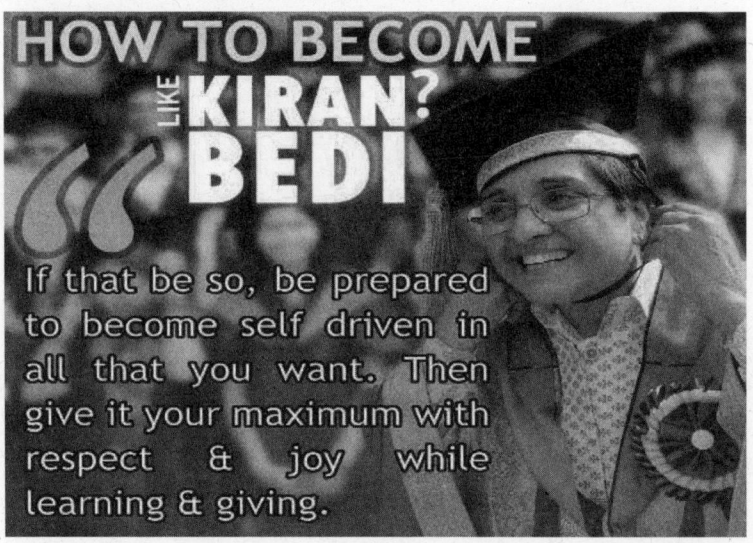

HOW TO BECOME LIKE KIRAN BEDI?

If that be so, be prepared to become self driven in all that you want. Then give it your maximum with respect & joy while learning & giving.

PART - B

THE INSPIRATIONAL CONNECT

As I finished working on the first part of this book I was inspired to delve deeper into the way Dr Kiran Bedi has worked as LG, learn more about the good practices she has adopted and encouraged and how it has helped not just her office at Rajnivas function better but also helped officers across ranks and hierarchies to improve the functioning of their offices.

Here is a leader who believed in team work, in transparency, in collaboration, in communication and, most of all, cutting across hierarchies and being accessible to all. "When I began my tenure as LG even in Rajnivas I found that I did not have a team who was working together, but individuals, each of whom are brilliant in their field, working by themselves. This is when I realised my first step would be to bring them together and encourage them to be a team and work together," says Dr Bedi. And that is how she formed Team Rajnivas.

This team comprises of her OSD (former secretary) Theva Neethi Dhas, Private Secretary R. Sridharan, Assistant Secretary S.D. Sundaresan, ADC S. Karthigayan, Comptroller Ms Asha Gupta, PRO J. Kumaran and Chief Grievance Officer

S. Bascarane. The team has functioned as the think tank, led by Dr Bedi herself. Impressed by their work, I interviewed them on how they saw these good practices evolve and how they have benefitted from them.

What I discovered in this process of talking to them was a remarkable model of governance which not just governments but any organisation can easily learn and adopt. A model that is based on team work and transparency and rides on the strength of communication and collaboration, all driven by the kindness of a leader who believed she was here fora purpose.

As a leader she is someone who brings in, what she believes in and what she wants, into alignment with what she does and this clearly is a hallmark of her integrity. What drives her passion to work is not being hungry for power or for accolades, but it is sheer sense of duty, of principles and in working with a purpose for which she has been given this position. "This is my duty and I must give it my 100 per cent" is her belief. It is awe inspiring to see a leader who is a perfect combination of a kind heart, sharp mind, brave spirit, always going the extra mile to serve her country and society.

Let me take you through each of these good practices and present to you a model that is the product of years of experience of a visionary leader. Dr Kiran Bedi believes this is a model which, when replicated and followed by other governments, departments, offices and organisations, will prove to be very beneficial to them.

I thank Dr Kiran Bedi for giving me this opportunity and guiding me through every step of working on this book. What began as a gift for her 70th birthday has evolved into a book on governance, leadership and good practices driven by her kindness and generosity.

BEST PRACTICES

THE MODEL
- Teaming up people into a think tank: Forming Team Rajnivas and the 10 a.m. meeting
- Ushering in an era of openness: Rajnivas to People's Nivas

  A beacon of hope: Open house

  Where dreams come true: Visitors' hour

  Inspiring through films: Film series

  Engaging great minds: Leadership series

  When officers became teachers: Lecture series

  Appreciating culture: Art and culture series

  A feeling of togetherness: Celebrating festivals

  Building future leaders: Internships
- Living life beyond barriers: Moving out of the comfort zone – weekend morning rounds
- Motivating through mentorship
- Personalised learning experiences: One-to-One meeting

  Learning and guiding through office visits

- Discovering one's potential: Self-evaluation tests
- Strategising and goal setting: Weekly and monthly review meetings
- Confirming truths: Surprise/incognito visits
- Engaging and Enlightening: The use of communication and technology
  - The Rajnivas fourth estate: The creative team – social media and documentation
  - Connectivity with a purpose: Prosperous Puducherry WhatsApp group
  - Transparency at its best: Weekly disposal of files update
  - Connecting with common man: A monthly engagement – Monthly message to citizens
- Networking
  - Giving back to the community: Rajnivas outreach programme
  - Towards collaboration and improvement: Coopting human resources
- Appreciation with kindness
  - Expressing gratitude: Water rich – Swachchata hi Seva awards
  - Recognising persistent efforts: Front-runner awards
  - A motivation to perform better: Weekly awards for police and municipality penalties
  - Appreciation for Green Ambassadors

TEAMING UP PEOPLE AS A THINK THANK
FORMING TEAM RAJNIVAS AND THE 10 AM MEETING

LEADERSHIP NUGGET

Allow yourself to be a beginner. No one starts off being excellent women of history!

Good leaders constantly seek opportunities to learn. They respect and recognise their team and arecourageous enough to admit that they want to know more. Which is why they are always seeking more and creating opportunities to know them directly

— Dr Kiran Bedi

@The Kiran Bedi:- #Team Rajnivas @ 10Am -ideates, identifies, plans, reviews, connects, To serve Puducherry better each single day @Rashtrapati Bhvn @ PMO India

25 May 2017

When Dr Kiran Bedi took over as LG, what she brought with her was her 40 years of experience as a cop, her administrative acumen coupled with her intense passion to serve her nation. Even as a cop she believed that policing stood for the power to correct, the power to prevent and the power to get things done rather than the power to punish. As an LG she came in with the belief that she was here on a mission to serve Puducherry and make it the most prosperous union territory in the country.

"Madam firmly believes in team work and even before she took oath as LG, she convened a meeting of secretaries and clearly explained her vision of being here as an administrator. What followed was an extension of something she has been practicing for years as a cop and so one of the first steps she took was to form the Team Rajnivas and start the 10 a.m. meetings," says Theva Neethi Dhas, her former secretary, currently serving as OSD.

True to the nugget quoted here, she allowed herself to be a beginner. To understand her team members better and to create an opportunity to know them better, to collaborate and work with them and to encourage them to be a team, she evolved the concept of the 10 a.m. meeting.

"Ma'am has been used to a structure of morning meetings from her days of policing. During her last posting in BPRD she used to have 9 a.m. meetings so when she came in here as LG, she called the entire team, introduced herself and explained to them how she has always followed the practice of having morning meetings. She asked them what time would be convenient to them and they said 10 a.m. That is how the 10 a.m. meetings began," says Dr Amrita Bahl, former OSD to LG.

The different departments of Rajnivas were working like silos until May 2016. They all met very rarely, maybe just once or twice in a year. Each department had its own working style and experts worked there to accomplish specific tasks.

It was indeed difficult for the vertical structures of departments to coordinate action and adapt to change.

Dr Bedi knew that breaking these silos and stovepipes was of no use. Instead of trying to eliminate the silos, she tried to connect them all effectively. The 10 a.m. meeting became a platform to connect them all.

The meeting is held daily, except on public holidays, and is made up of short briefings on anything important that is going on.

To make the work rendezvous more effective, Dr Bedi adopted virtual meetings with other departments.

The 10 a.m. meetings follow a clear agenda and each pending item is discussed and followed up thoroughly. Meetings are used to brainstorm on different issues or ideas, not to lecture or transmit information in a top-down manner. Each participant is an observer as well and helps to give new perspectives.

All meetings are well-recorded for reference and accountability.

"This meeting enabled each of us to understand our roles better and also to understand each other's strengths, to ideate, to envision, to collectively think, to execute and also follow up on all the work that was planned for," adds Neethi Dhas.

Typically, the 10 a.m. meeting involves identifying issues, setting priorities, reviewing press clippings and calling for action based on them, monitoring grievances and progress of work and tasks identified the previous day or during earlier meetings and setting the agenda for the day ahead. "The 10 a.m. meeting brought a whiff of freshness and innovation in the work culture. Initially we had officers from other departments join the meetings and we also connected with other regions of Puducherry – Mahe, Yanam and Karaikal – over video-conferencing. But due to various issues which came up, the 10 a.m. meetings, from being a larger footprint, evolved into an in-house think tank meeting," says R. Sreedhar private secretary to LG, who recalls that no LG hadever called earlier for such meetings involving officials. These meetings have definitely been a great learning experience for all the team members.

"I had never heard of the 10 a.m. meeting before I became part of the Team Rajnivas a few months ago. The meetings have a fixed agenda, but it is more like a family meet where we discuss all important matters, understand our roles and this helps to keep all of us on the same wavelength and also to know what the expected outcomes of each action should be. We also have our moments of fun. The meetings have been a huge learning experience for me," says S.D. Sundaresan, additional secretary to LG.

The news clippings are brought to this meeting in four folders, one for English clippings, one for Tamil, one for news you need to know from across the world and one for press releases from PIB (Press Information Bureau) pertaining to all news from the Government of India. "We work as a team in the morning to compile these news clippings which are presented to the honourable LG and the team and during the 10 a.m. meeting we pick up significant clippings and discuss them, send out action requests to concerned departments and clippings pertaining to grievances are given to the chief grievance officer," says J. Kumaran, the PRO at Rajnivas.

This 10 a.m. meeting, which has been providing synergy, creativity, cohesion and harmony, certainly has all the ingredients for good governance. The team does have its lighter moments every day and it is the kindness of Dr Kiran Bedi in guiding and mentoring the team at every step which helped each of them harness their strengths and give their best.

Led by a leader who is open to ideas and learning, who believes in transparency and participative team spirit Team Rajnivas, through these 10 a.m. meetings, has evolved into an action oriented, consensus driven team that has been able to bring about a marked change in the administration of Puducherry.

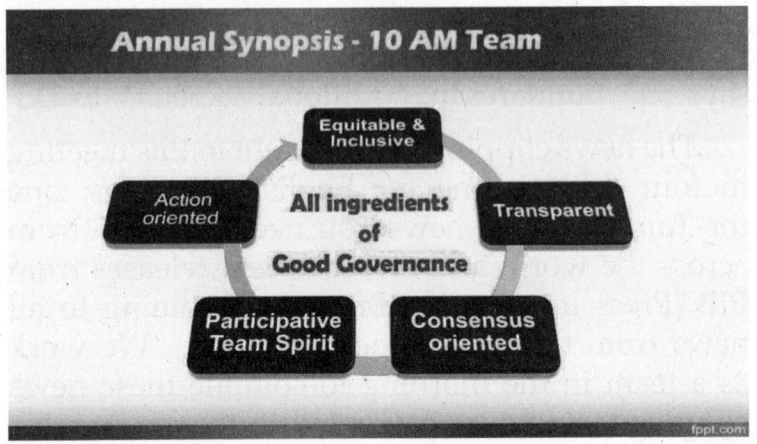

With a team at Rajnivas in place working as a think tank with her, ideating with the same infectious energy and kindness that she has, starting initiatives that would open up Rajnivas and make her more accessible was the next step in line for Dr Bedi and so Rajnivas became a people's nivas.

KEY TAKEAWAYS/ MANAGEMENT LESSONS

As a leader pay heed to your inner voice focusing on all four paradigms – spirit, body, heart and mind, and this will help in strategising your leadership goals

Rather than breaking a silo, encourage team spirit and team work.

Allow yourself to be a beginner, to understand your team and to encourage them to set goals and work on their respective strengths.

USHERING IN AN ERA OF OPENNESS: MAKING RAJNIVAS A PEOPLE NIVAS

LEADERSHIP NUGGET

People always want to see an engaged leadership. Leadership must stand firm in situations where it needs to, with a high energy focus round-the-year and round-the-clock.

— Dr Kiran Bedi

In Open House at RajNivas, anyone can come to RajNivas on declared dates & timings without appointment. Can come to greet, meet & express an issue. We also use this occasion to recognise & reward for shared inspiration.
@NewIndianXpress @PMOIndia @ANI @rashtrapatibhvn @HMOIndia

11 June 2019

⇀ A BEACON OF HOPE: OPEN HOUSE

> @TheKiranBedi- In Open House at RajNivas, anyone can come to RajNivas on declared dates & timings without appointment. Can come to greet, meet & express an issue. We also use this occasion to recognise & reward for shared inspiration. @NewIndianXpress @ANI @rashtrapatibhvn @PMOIndia @HMOIndia
>
> 11 June 2019

A firm believer in the maxim, "The higher the position the more accessible it ought to be," Dr Kiran Bedi decided to start the practice of open house as soon as she took over as LG. This is an extension of what she had already practised as special secretary to Lt Governor of Delhi, Tejendra Khanna, way back in 1998.

Within days of taking over as LG, Dr Bedi started the open house at Rajnivas. She opened out the gates of Rajnivas, a building that was considered an ivory tower where even a bird could not fly through without permission. "When madam took over, she was in touch with only officers and the feedback we got from officers was all good, but when she began to step out and see the reality she realised that people needed to be heard and helped and that is how the concept of open house began," says S. Bascarane, Chief Grievance Officer at Rajnivas.

> **Meet Lt.Guv between 5-6pm without appointment**
>
> **Puducherry:** Lt Governor Kiran Bedi, who directed all the top officials in the union territory to allot one hour (5pm-6pm) to meet the general public and redress their grievances, has set an example by meeting people from June 1. People from all walks of life started visiting Raj Nivas, Lt Governor's official residence, between 5pm and 6pm, raising a wide range of issues before her without prior appointment. A foreigner, who made Puducherry her home, appreciated Bedi's goal to make Puducherry a prosperous territory. However, she insisted that its legacy of being a spiritual and peaceful town must be preserved. TNN ▶ **Continued on, P 2**

Initially, all through the week, the open house was held from 5 to 6 p.m. and 40 tokens were issued on a first-come-first-served basis, grievances were heard and solutions provided. But as work evolved, the open house timings were restricted to Monday to Wednesday, 5 to 7 p.m., and the same 40 tokens are issued. Records of all those coming with grievances are meticulously maintained and follow-ups are made for cases for which action is called. Wednesdays 6 to 7 p.m. is dedicated to both retired and serving government servants and Fridays are dedicated for open house through video conferencing with regions of Karaikal, Mahe and Yanam.

"The involvement of paralegals comprising of Lok Adalat, Family Counsellor from welfare department and Tahsildar from the survey departments has been immensely helpful and facilitates sorting of issues quickly," says Sreedhar, private secretary to LG.

The open house has dealt with complaints ranging from issues as serious as land grabbing as well as property disputes, corruption, family disputes, water issues and the even the medical admission issues, which were repeatedly brought to the notice of the LG. After the medical admission issues were raised in the open house, the LG visited the CENTAC office and the rest is history. Another area where the open house really helped was in the project "Water-rich Puducherry". The complaint of choked water channels came through open house, which led to field visits to inspect water channels, lakes and ponds and resulted in desilting them with the help of corporate social responsibility activities.

Open house has also helped bring back people stranded in places like the Middle-East where they were taken on the pretext of giving work and abused. With the help of the ministry of external affairs, the officials were able to bring back many people and unite them with their families.

Grievances are received through emails, WhatsApp and through other social media platforms as well. "In April 2017, when we launched the Rajnivas website, we incorporated a petition monitoring system into it to be able to attend to grievances more effectively. Every complaint received is acknowledged and the complainant receives a unique ID number for future correspondence through the preferred mode of communications such as SMS, email or paper. Once registered, these grievances are redressed by the respective departments, while the Lieutenant Governor's Secretariat monitors them. Grievances marked confidential are accessed and dealt with strictly by the Lieutenant Governor's Confidential Desk," says Bascarane.

> @TheKiranbedi: This is how petitions r being addressed/reviewed daily/shared on Whataspp Recvd from all sources r hosted in computerised PMS system. Coordinated by Mr Srinivas, Addl Sec, RajNivas & Dr Bascar Chief Grievances Officer with nodal officers. Petitioner satisfaction is checked.
>
> 22 March 2018

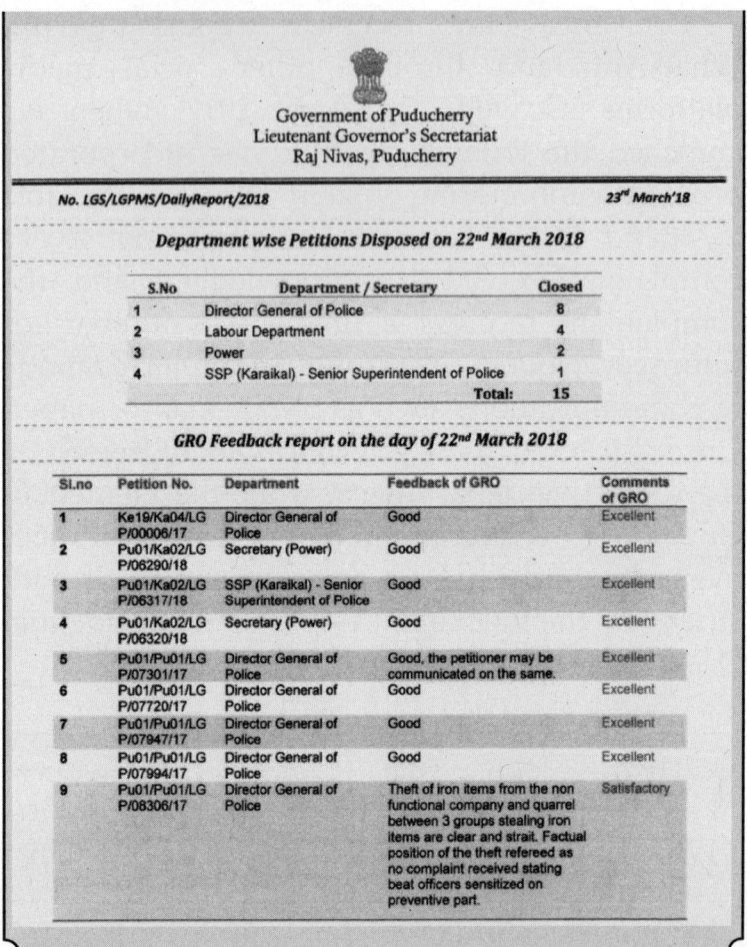

A forum that works with an absolutely humanitarian approach, where people are heard directly by the Lieutenant Governor herself, open house has emerged as the top best-practice of Rajnivas. A leader who is eager to serve rather than make people wait to be served, Dr Kiran Bedi is a beacon of hope for the people of Puducherry.

They walk into Rajnivas and are greeted with utmost kindness. They are made to sit comfortably and are even given tea and biscuits, which they can pick up for themselves from the portico as they await their turn to be heard. Once they are into LG's office, she personally greets them with so much of love that despite not knowing their language, they feel that here is someone who is really here to help them and their problems will be solved.

A SYNOPSIS OF GRIEVANCES RECEIVED

Year	LGPMS(LG'S PETITION MONITORING SYSTEM)	WhatsApp	Open House	Total
2016	5,921	0	2,796	8,717
2017	8,590	1,721	2,598	12,909
2018	8,068	2,773	3,512	14,353
2019 (as on 31-5-2019)	2,551	834	726	4,111
Total	25,130	5,328	9,632	40,090

If people have a chance to walk up to their LG with their grievances and she listens to them and helps them with utmost kindness, then the millions of people for whom Dr Bedi is a role model also get a chance to meet their icon and interact with her during the visitors' hour.

WHERE DREAMS COME TRUE
VISITORS HOUR

@TheKiranBedi: Raj Nivas opened to visitors from today 12-1.30 PM. 1st batch of visitors came by registering on http://RajNivas.py.gov.in Welcome to RajNivas

1 May 2017

Dr Kiran Bedi, as LG, always knew Rajnivas was not just going to be her residence-cum-office but also a space for her to connect with people and so she instantly opened up the gates of Rajnivas. "Internally, the Rajnivas was on a journey of churning to becoming a People's Nivas. Home and Office to the Lieutenant Governor – the First Citizen of Puducherry – was the only way this stately building was known to us, the staff as well as to the outsiders. Could there be any other dimension? How ignorant we were was to be proved in the months ahead," says Asha Gupta the comptroller of household at Rajnivas.

What started with 4 p.m. appointments followed by open house eventually evolved into a visitors' hour (started 1 May 2017) every day from 12.30 to 1.30 p.m. where people come more to meet the iconic Dr Kiran Bedi rather than to see the heritage building. "I am only one of the residents here at Rajnivas and this building belongs to all. Everyone must have an opportunity to see the beautiful heritage building and experience its splendour," says Dr Bedi with her child-like enthusiasm as she meets groups of visitors every day who, make a beeline to take photographs with their icon. What could better elucidate the leadership nugget quoted above on engaged leadership? She is open to not just meeting people but also listening to their ideas and views, and immediately gives them opportunity to work with her team. Many visitors are today partnering with Rajnivas on CSR activities. Children get to sit on her chair because she believes this will inspire them to become LGs in the future. "Inspire to Aspire" is her mantra and kids enjoy their two minutes of fame sitting on the LG's chair.

"Request for visits poured in from visitors, students, international tourists and groups of every category. This became a daily feature at noon at the Rajnivas. The Lt Governor's chambers were to see more firsts of sorts. Dr Kiran Bedi welcomed children and students to sit on the official chair at the Lt Governor's desk. Visitors always left with a gift (pencils, books, memorabilia), a smile and amazing memories of having met their mega icon in person; and to see that she was so down-to-earth, impossibly simple and caring," says Asha Gupta.

Visitors come with gifts but "recycle" is Dr Kiran Bedi's mantra and all the gifts coming in would go into the LG's gift cupboard and be promptly presented to others. "These gifts are not being given to Kiran Bedi, they are being given to the Lieutenant Governor and belong to the office. So I don't take any of them for myself but put them away in the cupboard.Igive them to visitors and also to officers for their good performance. I give shawls to our Swachchata workers who work hard to keep our city clean,"says Dr Kiran Bedi.

Till date over 450 batches of visitors have come to Rajnivas, ranging from students to groups of women to foreigners and even tourists who are holidaying in Puducherry. The visitor's hour is one of the many initiatives taken by Dr Kiran Bedi which has made Rajnivas into a People's Nivas or Lok Nivas, as she refers to it.

At a college event Dr Bedi saw a mobile LED screen and decided that she would procure one, convert the Rajnivas lawns into an open theatre for children and show them inspirational movies as part of the Rajnivas film series. It would be another opportunity for them to come to Rajnivas and go back inspired.

LG Oath Taking

Oath Administered to MLAs

Monthly Briefing with Secretaries

Meeting With Chief Secretary

10 AM meeting

One on One Meeting with Juliet Pushpa, Secretary Law

Field Visit to Department

Open House

10 Am Team and Creative Team

Film Series

Leadership Series

Lecture Series - Sadhguru

Lecture Series Dr Mariazeena Johnson

Inspiring to Aspire

Iftaar Party

Pongal celebrations

Front Runner Awards

Self Evaluation Test

Self Defense Class At Rajnivas

Thanking Swachchata Workers At Rajnivas

Weekly Awards For Traffic Penalties

Bus Ride For Water Rich Puducherry

Swachch Cycle Rally

Desilted Water Channel

Honouring Swachhata Workers With Shawls

Networking And Coopting Women Leaders

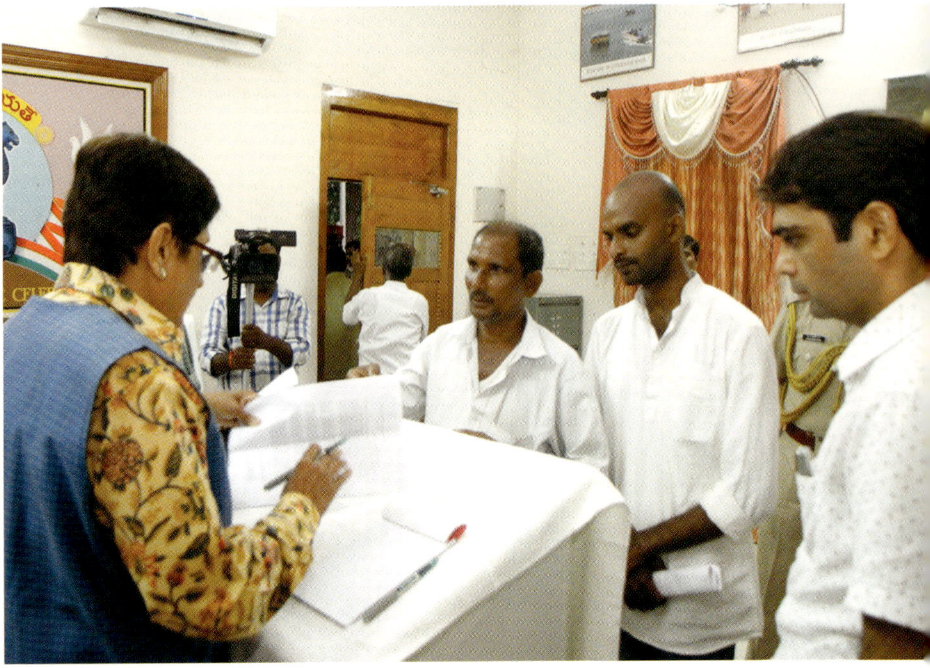

Yanam Open House

Yanam School Visit

Coopting Women Leaders

Self Evaluation Tests

Mission Green Puducherry

INSPIRING THROUGH FILMS: RAJNIVAS FILM SERIES

> @TheKiranBedi-
>
> Sowing seeds for inspired leadership. Also optimally using resources which belong to the people. #RajNivas delivering its own potential..
>
> A new kind of breakthru where #RajNiwas inspires children thru screening of Award Winning Films. They r r future @RashtrapatiBhvn@PMOIndia
>
> 25 February 2017

Dr Kiran Bedi, in anattemptto use all the resources ofRajnivas optimally to inspire children to become future leaders, started the Rajnivas Film Series in February 2017. Rajnivas has the most beautiful lawns which could easily be converted into an open-air theatre and that's exactly what was done. Once a month, on Saturday evenings, children came with parents, teachers and friends to watch an inspiring movie followed by an interaction with the honourable LG herself.

"Inspiring children was to be a focus of Rajnivas. So in the Rajnivas Film Series, award-winning and educational films were screened for special children from Destitute Homes, Government and other select institutions. As part of the film series, 13 movies have been viewed by 7,300 persons," says Asha Gupta, the comptroller at Rajnivas, who was instrumental in organising these film screenings.

The first film shown in this series was *Kaka Muttai* and later films like *Gandhi*, *Life of Pi*, *MS Dhoni*, *Chak De India*, *Madela* and so on have been screened. "The children's film series has been our way of investing in the future, sowing seeds of an inspired generation of Indians. I always interact with the children after the film screening and tell them how they need to grow up to be strong leaders of the future," says Dr Kiran Bedi. She once even told the children that whoever came first in class would get an opportunity to sit on the LG's chair!

@Lgov_Puducherry- #RajNivasFilmSeries: HLG @thekiranbedi encourages young kids to come 1st in class & as reward get a photo clicked sitting on HLG's seat

To further inspire the students, Dr Bedi also facilitated a tour of the heritage building for them. The splendour of the building and the inspiring interaction with the honourable LG leaves a lasting impact on the minds of these children.

For every screening, a new group of students was invited, not just to watch the inspiring movie but was also motivated to become future public officials, administrators, academicians, sports person and, above all, good human beings.

Dr Bedi wanted to use the facilities at Rajnivas optimally and one of the ways she thought was to invite speakers and open the event to public by invitation. Thus emerged the Rajnivas lecture series.

ENGAGING GREAT MINDS: RAJNIVAS LECTURE SERIES

@Lgov_ Puducherry- Launching #The RajNivasLectureSeries, an endeavor to engage citizens on #ThoughtLeadership. @RajeevPeshawria speaks on #Leadership Energy.

♡ 22 December 2016

The Rajnivas lecture series is an initiative by Dr Kiran Bedi to engage citizens of Puducherry on thought leadership through a series of interactive sessions by eminent speakers from the fields of history, art, leadership, literature, management, science, culture, health, spiritually and so on.

"Rajnivas hosts a lecture series where eminent speakers deliver talks on varied subjects ranging from leadership, management, history, philosophy, etc. The blessed presence of Sadhguru Jaggi Vasudev, the investigative fervour of Maxwell Pereira, practices of excellence by Rajeev Peshawaria, the Vision of Debashish Chatterjee, the Vedic relevance by Jaya Rao, Swami Radhanath Swami brought in unparalleled knowledge to citizens of Puducherry," says Asha Gupta.

The dining hall in Rajnivas was converted into a lecture hall where people were provided with food for thought. The first lecture was delivered by Rajeev Peshawaria on leadership qualities and the invitees included ministers, elected representatives, public officials and academicians. "I was incredibly fortunate and honoured to be invited for the inaugural RajNivas lecture series. This is the first time I have witnessed a government leader opening up an official residence to the public in the way Puducherry Rajnivas has done and continues to do so. Leaders from all over the world can learn from this. The Rajnivas team has shown to the world that the real meaning of leadership is serving," says Rajeev Peshawaria.

The next lecture was by Dr P. Raja, who narrated the history of Puducherry through selectfolk tales.The venue for this was the Rajnivas lawns so that the youth could be invited and the lawns could provide space for a larger audience. Sadhguru Jaggi Vasudev spoke on making of a nation, Jaya Row spoke on spirituality and Maxwell Pereira spoke on the gruesome tandoor murder. Such lectures have been a part of the lecture series and have helped to connect people from divergent sections in a constructive and productive manner. They have also laid the foundation for strong leadership practices.

Noticing the potential in each of her officers, Dr Bedi decided to encourage them to share their best practices and experiences which would enable other officers to learn from them. So she started the Rajnivas leadership series.

WHEN OFFICERS BECAME TEACHERS: RAJNIVAS LEADERSHIP SERIES

> @TheKiranBedi- RajNivas Leadership series.. Today it was on Sustainable Development Goals and Puducherry-The Way Forward. Superb presentation.. Thanku Candu. @AshwaniKumar_92@ DrJitendraSingh
>
> 13 April 2018

When a leader believes in team work, in ideating together and in coopting leaders and grooming them to be team leaders, then emerges an initiative like the Rajnivas leadership series. This, again, is an extension of the persona of Dr Bedi who had been a teacher before becoming a cop. She was never a teacher who stood behind a desk and took a one-sided class. She always involved the students and made them teach because she believed that the best way to learn is to teach and so her classes were always interactive.

"The leadership series and the lecture series are both an extension of the persona of Dr Kiran Bedi who believes in both learning from her teams and teaching them. The leadership series encourages officers to choose a topic of their choice related to the departments they belong to, ponder of the policies, rules, deficiencies and in a way makes them revise their work. When they present their lecture in the presence of their team members as well as other departments, it helps them share the best practices they use, get feedback and improve their work. Like they say, the best way to learn is to teach, and this forum is the best opportunity to teach and to learn," says Theva Neethi Dhas.

The leadership series is basically a platform for sharing best practices, work experiences and continuous inhouse training. It leads to orienting administration towards ups killing and realigning its professional capital for optimal efficiency and reinforced team spirit.

Officers from various departments have been a part of this leadership series. The first talk was given by Mr A. Anbarasu followed by officers like Mr Candavelou, Mr G. Srinivas, who was formerly the additional secretary to LG and instrumental in implementing GST in Puducherry, to name a few.

"Leadership series is a first of its kind initiative at Rajnivas, Puducherry. I was excited but at the same time tensed, when Honourable Lt Governor informed me that I should share my experiences in the next round of leadership series. I made a brief presentation on implementation of GST in Puducherry and some practices adopted in commercial taxes department for providing quality service and check tax evasion. Apart from sharing,

I feel the leadership series is an opportunity to learn from the lectures delivered by experienced officers, which are immensely useful as we progress in our career," says G. Srinivas.

When every part of Rajnivas was being used for programmes like film screenings to giving lectures and even celebrating festivals, then why not convert the reception area into an art gallery?

APPRECIATING ART AND CULTURE: RAJNIVAS ART AND CULTURE SERIES

> Lgov_Puducherry- HLG @thekiranbedi kicked off the Raj Nivas Art and Culture Series with a photo exhibition. On display were photos of the best moments of #FIFA#WorldCup2018 by S.Sukumar. The series will roll out a wide range of Cultural and Art Programs in the coming days.
>
> 6 August 2018

Dr Kiran Bedi as an LG has not left any avenue unexplored and she has even promoted art and culture at Rajnivas through the art and culture Series. This is an initiative to promote performing arts, visual arts, fine arts and other forms of art. It aims to promote traditional local art and culture forms and showcase works of eminent artistes.

The lobby of Rajnivas transforms into an art gallery where the art works of different artistes are beautifully displayed and visitors to Rajnivas catch a glimpse of them as they wait to meet the honourable lieutenant governor.

"In the Art and Culture series, the gallery spaces of this heritage building were exhibition backdrops for creative and performing arts. The paintings by the inmates of the prison, photographs of one thousand days of Puducherry under Dr Kiran Bedi and of course a series of photographs taken by Dr Kiran Bedi, Vedic chanting, wildlife in urban forests, are some dimensions of Art and Culture Series over its nine editions," says Asha Gupta

The fourth edition of the series, which was very special, showcased works created as part of the inmates' reformation programme at the Kalapet Ashram. The exhibition was titled "Reviving Hope" and 21 artworks were displayed. The training, which started off as a mundane activity, turned out to be a huge encouragement to the inmates who brought out some splendid creations with the help of the authorities and the support of the CSR partners.

Other exhibitions like that on water-rich Puducherry, wildlife of urban trails and not to forget the pictures taken by honourable LG herself during her morning exercise hours in the lawns of Rajnivas have all been great highlights of the Rajnivas Art and Culture series.

This series has been one of the key initiatives which has helped transform Rajnivas into a People's Nivas.

At Rajnivas all festivals are celebrated with full fervour with officers and guests.

A FEELING OF TOGETHERNESS:
CELEBRATING FESTIVALS

> @TheKiranbedi-Raj Nivas welcomes visitors inside RajNivas premises on New Year Eve. As it did on Diwali, Jan 26th, Aug 15 and Pongal. There has been a steady stream of visitors since 6PM... The Fountain is playing also with light instrumental music. Visitors have been enjoying taking photos..
>
> ♡ 31 December 2017

At Rajnivas festivals are always celebrated with a lot of fervour. Dr Bedi's belief that every festival must be celebrated with the people, drives Team Rajnivas to plan these celebrations in the most traditional way. If it is Pongal, even a bullock cart comes in, rangoli competition is conducted for the adults and children take part in bun-eating competitions, apart from the entertainment and the food that is served. For Christmas, Santa Claus comes in and along with him comes a group to sing carols and visitors get to eat cake, too. During the month of Ramadaan, ifthar party is held and Dr Bedi herself is a part of this celebration where she greets the people, prays with them and offers them food. Even a festival like Basant Panchami is celebrated at Rajnivas when children from the Gurukul nearby come and chant slokas.

"While the regional Pongal festival was celebrated with family members of the Rajnivas fraternity, for Christmas were invited children from special homes, nuns, senior citizens and choirs for carol gaiety. Ifthar in Rajnivas had in the past meant a splurge of non-vegetarian fare, unlimited guests and of course considerable expenditure. With these winds of change, ifthar at Rajnivas became an evening of prayer and symbolic breaking of the fast. While austerity was in, courtesy and hospitality were given precedence," says Asha Gupta.

On days like the Independence Day, Republic Day and New Year Eve, in the evening the lawns are beautifully lit up and visitors are allowed to walk in and enjoy the beauty and take photos. This is the way Rajnivas has been promoting a sense of togetherness and fraternity under the kind leadership of Dr Kiran Bedi.

Inspired leadership is Dr Bedi's belief and what better way to do it than allow interns to come and experience working at the Lt Governor's secretariat?

BUILDING FUTURE LEADERS:
INTERNS FOR SOCIAL LEADERSHIP – RAJNIVAS YOUTH ENGAGEMENT PROGRAMME

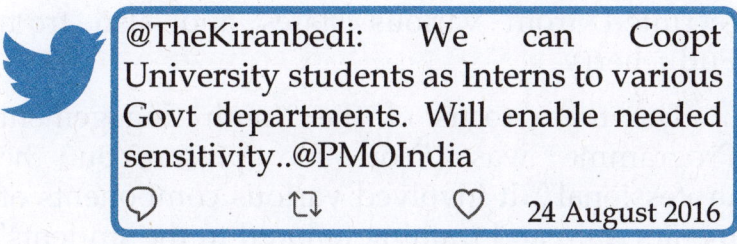

@TheKiranbedi: We can Coopt University students as Interns to various Govt departments. Will enable needed sensitivity..@PMOIndia

24 August 2016

Dr Kiran Bedi has been a role model and inspiration for millions of youth across the country and the globe. And when she decides to open the doors of Rajnivas to youth with a motive to create young leaders, then emerges a programme like the Rajnivas Youth Engagement Programme.

What started off as a programme where interns came in, turn-by-turn, perhaps a maximum of three to four interns being a part of it at a time, grew into a full time youth engagement programme in the summer of 2019 where 23 interns came in to be groomed as future leaders.

Rajnivas Youth Engagement Programme is a comprehensive developmental programme intended to provide students with experience in our dynamic work environment that was expected to enhance their educational goals and help shape their career choices.

Rajnivas received an overwhelming response to the Youth Engagement Programme. For the summer internship call of 2019, several applications were received, all seeking to serve the country through attending a productive internship. All applications were evaluated and the best students recruited from various states and also from Puducherry.

The main focus of the Youth Engagement Programme was "You the person,You the professional". It involved various components of mentor ship and training tailored to the students' education, experience, and interests that may help them to nurture and balance the personal and professional lives. From Interns' Lectures to Culinary Sessions and Educational Visits as well as Field Visits, the programme was designed to stimulate students by making them undergo various projects under the direct supervision of the Lt Governor and other senior team members of the Rajnivas.

"I believe every government office must open up their doors for such internship programmes so the youth get exposure to how the government offices function, how policies are made.The offices, in turn, get new ideas from the youth who come in like a whiff of fresh air, bringing in the most innovative of thoughts and ideas," says Dr Kiran Bedi.

It is indeed a moment of pride for the youth to be face-to-face with their icon and role model and to be mentored by her is absolutely fabulous. "Please identify the purpose of your being here, the purpose of the line you are choosing for yourself and then work towards it," she tells them and guides them at every step personally. From sharing inspirational thoughts to videos which would impact them to even gifting them alarm clocks and telling them "Wake up sleepy heads!" Dr Bedi left a lasting impact on the minds of these 23 young girls and boys who spent their summer interning at Rajnivas.

Truly all of these initiatives, be it the visitor's hour, the film series, lecture series, leadership series, internships or art and culture series, have all contributed to Rajnivas becoming a Peoples' Nivas or Lok Nivas. The open house has also helped it in becoming a Vishwas Nivas. And there could not be a better example for engaged leadership than these initiatives taken by Dr Kiran Bedi.

MANAGEMENT LESSON
The more successful leader you become the more chances that you may become less accessible. But remember that accessibility is the key to be an outstanding leader. Make a concentrated effort to be accessible to those who need you and be available to them.

- Keep a fixed time in your office to meet people (to hear grievances if in government services).
- Encourage activities which will make your office space more accessible and also encourage future leadership.

"I am not here to sit inside the Rajnivas so the moment I get a chance, I step out," says Dr Bedi who is totally field oriented and believes in going to the problem and solving it. That is her fixed agenda every weekend morning.

LIVING LIFE BEYOND BARRIERS: MOVING OUT OF THE COMFORT ZONE – WEEKEND MORNING ROUNDS

> **LEADERSHIP NUGGET**
> #TeamRajNivas continues to step out of "comfort zone" on a regular basis to enable keep diff segments of society enthused to realise and value their roles and presence. This is an important requisite for all leadership-responsibilities.
>
> — Dr Kiran Bedi

> @TheKiranbedi-Mission #GreenPuducherry' launched as a part of 70th birthday today. Thank residents of Kangan Lake area for facilitating. Hereafter all weekend rounds stand dedicated to planting trees to keep the Green Puducherry Mission going. Today was 219 th morning round for #TeamRajnivas
>
> 9 June 2019

Someone rightly said, "Great things never came from staying in comfort zones," and true to this maxim, Team Rajnivas, under the leadership of Dr Kiran Bedi, has dedicated its weekend mornings to field visits to areas that require attention.

Field visits have always been part of the working style of Dr Kiran Bedi who even as a cop was always visible on the streets. "I started my weekend morning rounds from the very first weekend of my responsibility here as Lt Governor. My first round came as a response to Hon'ble Speaker's grievance from his constituency about choked water drains. And he bringing in the resident's delegation to visit me. They wanted a solution. On their request I went to the residential colony and saw it in need of strong intervention. The second request for a field visit came from MLA Mr Laxmi Narayan for Grand Canal cleaning. I went with him too and saw for myself that the situation was pretty bad. Reality on ground too may be quite different. I felt that to improve things faster I will have to step out of comfort zone and do regular field visits. I chose weekend mornings because it's my own time and pace. Office work does not have to wait," says Dr Kiran Bedi who has diligently led these visits every weekend, sometimes going on a bicycle it, sometimes going by car or even by bus, with the entire team. Her visits have truly been game changers. From helping desilt water channels to make Puducherry water rich to reviving lakes to creating awareness on helmets and swachch cycle rallies, these weekend rounds have been very impactful and will be always remembered in the annals of the administrative history of Puducherry.

"These weekend rounds have been an offshoot of grievances received in the open house or received through emails and other social media or sometimes even through news items. ADC informs the MLA of the area about the visit and then the team goes along with madam on these weekend rounds. The spot is visited, the problem looked into, assessed, solution sought and the concerned departments are informed to take action immediately. Follow ups to check on the action taken are also made during these weekend rounds," says Theva Neethi Dhas.

Till October 2019 the team has done about 234 weekend rounds and they have been able to revive lakes like the Velrampet lake, Kanagan lake, Ossudu lake to name a few; choked water channels, canals and drains have been desilted and cleaned up; the beach has been partially revived and villages have been visited. These rounds have also helped Dr Kiran Bedi and her team take stock of the sanitation issues in the city and helped them work towards a Swachh Puducherry.

"Weekend rounds can be defined as an initiative to reach out to people at the grass root level to know and address the needs of common man. People look forward for visit of Honourable Lt Governor as change for the better is imminent and their grievances are addressed," says G.

Srinivas, former additional secretary to LG who accompanied her on most weekend rounds.

Ths year on her 70th birthday Dr Kiran Bedi announced that from now onwards her weekend rounds would be towards making Puducherry a green Puducherry and every weekend she would be planting saplings along river beds and in public places. People from all walks of life were welcome to join her in these rounds to plant trees provided they brought their own seeds and saplings. She began this green Puducherry mission by planting a sapling along the Kanagan lake.

"These weekend rounds have definitely been an eye opener and a game changer but would have been much more beneficial if we had a welcoming elected government. People here have always wanted a proactive governor and these weekend rounds with her have been a great learning experience and a treasure to cherish. Although political frictions have been coming in the way, madam has not allowed these to deter her from going on these weekend rounds," says R. Sridharan.

Puducherry will never forget the LG who was seen cycling in the streets, waving to people, stopping to thank Swachchata workers and at times even wearing gloves and picking up garbage herself. "It would be a luxury to sit in my bed and sip tea early morning on weekends, but I chose work over luxury because problems cannot be solved if I sit inside Rajnivas. I needed to go out and see the problem myself and when we leaders start walking/biking the streets, the issues automatically start getting attended to. That is why it is important to step out of the comfort zone," says Dr Kiran Bedi.

Wherever she travelled, she never missed a weekend round. She cycled in Chandigarh for Rally for Rivers and in Karaiakal where she camped for a week to take stock of the situation there. She even made headlines when she scaled the wall of a building to check the premises.

"It is after 25 years that I cycled during a weekend round with madam. I joined her team just a few months ago and working with her has been such a huge learning experience. Her energy levels are contagious and the way she appreciates and applauds the smallest of achievements is worth admiring and emulating," says S.D. Sundaresan, Additional Secretary to LG.

These weekend rounds have helped to boost public confidence in the officials and in the government's ability to resolve issues.

MANAGEMENT LESSON

Field trips are considered the most important moments of learning and when a leader makes regular field trips, he becomes more visible and this results in positive outcomes.

All government officers must have fixed time for field visits. They must walk/bike down the streets and in villages to attend to grievances.

A kind leader believes in both learning and in mentoring her peers and juniors. The same was with Dr Bedi who evolved a pattern of meetings and department visits to improve functioning of Puducherry administration.

MOTIVATING THROUGH MENTORSHIP: MENTORING, SELF-EVALUATION AND APPRAISALS

> **LEADERSHIP NUGGET**
>
> A leader is constantly impacting. Everyone observes how he or she leads. How the leader expresses oneself through value systems in personal and professional responsibilities. Leaders to stay on course do regular self-audit with own selves. An audit which leads them towards self-correction and not self-reconciliation or giving up to wrongs or inadequacies.
>
> —Dr Kiran Bedi

PERSONALISED LEARNING EXPERIENCES: ONE-ON-ONE MEETINGS

> **@TheKiranBedi:**
>
> One on One meeting with Dir Env, Science & Tech & Coop Societies. Today she returned much improved from her earlier meeting on Sept 19th. On being appreciated & made to realise the value of her contribution she said, "We needed to have started this way from beginning of r career"
>
> 19 October 2018

Being a leader with extremely rich work experience and being a trainer at heart, Dr Kiran Bedi set out on the task of mentoring, training, orienting and motivating officials to perform better. This is how she evolved the concept of the one-on-one meetings where every morning at 9 a.m. she would meet an officer heading a particular department and try to understand their style of working, the issues they were facing and guide them how to improve their work so their departments could perform better.

"These one-on-one meetings helped the officers to express openly the issues they were facing which they may not be able to express in a joint meeting. Madam guides them based on her rich work experience and utilises her time and office to help them become better team leaders," says Theva Neethi Dhas.

The mentoring, steering and hand holding during the briefings have helped to improve administrative practices used in grievance redressal, departmental policies, drawing out standard operating procedures, understanding the importance of field visits, connecting with subordinate staff, conducting follow-up meetings and scheduling open house sessions.

Dr Kiran Bedi used this forum not just to mentor the officials but also to learn from them the good practices they followed in their respective departments which were worth emulating.

As she held these one-on-one meetings at Rajnivas, Dr Bedi realised the need to also visit these departments to understand their functioning better. So she would go every morning at 9 a.m. to a department to make all the difference.

LEARNING AND GUIDING: FIELD VISITS TO DEPARTMENTS

@TheKiranBedi- This morning onsite Office visit was to Dept of labour. They were seen to be using technology better. Areas for further progress were identified to aid, 'ease of doing business' by improving internal coord. They shall take a self evaluation test on Feb 16 to help refresh/upgrade

25 January 2019

Following the one-on-one meetings with officials in her office, Dr Kiran Bedi decided to start visiting theses offices so she could interact with the entire team, see their office set-up, how they were functioning and guide them on how they could improve their working.

Sharp 9.30 a.m. she would leave Rajnivas with her team and head out to visit a department and spend sufficient time there trying to understand how work wenton there. "Madam always begins with what you have and during her inspections she would encourage and guide departments on how they could perform better with whatever resources they have," says R. Sridharan.

These visits helped to bridge hierarchies, provide insights into practical aspects of work methodology and give clarity of working aids and environments in the respective departments. These visits also served as platforms to synchronise pending inter-departmental issues. There was an impetus on use of technology for better delivery of services.

These field visits helped Dr Kiran Bedi connect with the last-line staff in the departments and in many instances even connect with the public who wereat the office for getting work done, like people visiting the transport department for licences, to understand what problems they were facing.

Back from the inspection, Dr Bedi would record her inspection notes and share them with the respective groups before getting on to her next meeting. Her lessons to the departments and post-inspection notes are worthy of being called management lessons.

Here is a post-inspection note written by her after visiting the department of labour.

> This morning on-site office visit was to Dept of labour.
>
> This Dept deals with issues of employment exchange, skill development, labour issues, inspectorate of factories, boilers and shops and establishment.

The visit was very reassuring in several areas being ably led by Mr E. Vallavan.

It's use of technology was seen to be very dynamic with future plans in place to further upgrade in a time bound manner.

The discussions with Staff comprising of labour officers, Inspectors and Health officers led to the following decisions for further progress in providing ease of business, skill development and employment generation.

- The employment exchange form to be modified to capture the data of preferred skill and choice of job orientation for the dept to know areas of focus for employment and skill dev.

- Also include in the form options of internship or voluntary services carried out by candidates, if any.

- Also incorporate the willingness of the applicants for any voluntary service for the labour Dept to sponsor names to factories/NGOs and institutions.

- The Dept shall prepare a comprehensive presentation of what they are doing in each vertical of their work and the roles of line departments who need to be work in tandem for a coordinated ease of doing business in Puducherry.

- The Dept shall link their study rooms with Rolland Library for information and guidance to persons visiting the exchange office, facility of which is already existing.
- Their self-evaluation test on laws and acts applicable to their work, shall be held at Rajnivas on 23 Feb at 9 a.m. This is to help them further refresh their legal and functional knowledge.

As she interacted with officers in the departments she visited, she noticed how important it was to make these officers go through self-evaluation tests not just to understand their own strengths and weakness but also to read and learn more about the departments they work for.

DISCOVERING ONE'S POTENTIAL: SELF-EVALUATION TESTS

> @TheKiranBedi: The practice of self evaluation tests for key officers of respective departments is proving productive. It is encouraging and instilling the habit of team+self learning.
>
> 26 February 2019

When Dr Kiran Bedi visited the department of social welfare and interacted with the staff, she was rather appalled to note that most of the staff there was not aware of the laws about issues they were dealing with. This was when she decided to start the practice of self-evaluation tests and told them she would come back two weeks later and give them a test. They all needed to read up about all the laws pertaining to their departments and be ready to take the test.

This evolved into a system of self-evaluation for officers of all departments to improve delivery of public services. Soon she began having these tests in the durbar hall of Rajnivas. The morning would begin with an informal breakfast, followed by the test.

These in-house evaluation modules aim to refresh as well as update knowledge on latest interpretation of laws, amendments, instructions and orders. The module comprised three sections, the first section being the officer's personal particulars, the second being a subject-based questionnaire and the third being a SWOT analysis by each individual. "This initiative helps the officers to improve their knowledge, it encouraged them to read more and they have all been appreciative of these tests as they go back better informed," says R. Sridhar, who has been instrumental in helping Dr Kiran Bedi conduct these tests.

This initiative did face a lot of political opposition but Dr Bedi remained firm on her words and the tests went on without any hindrance. "Due to lack of regular and mid-career training, the officers lack updated knowledge on rules, regulations and procedures. LG's secretariat has consistently advised secretaries to government and heads of department to arrange for regular training to the staff and officers. Thankfully, the feedback from officers who went through a test based on self-study is very positive. They have stated that they have felt more confident. This underscores the need for sustained efforts," said Dr Bedi and also reiterated that the LG, as administrator, was fully competent to make sure that such training programmes are carried out properly as per legal provisions.

Review meetings have always been a part of Dr Bedi's style of working for a long time, so the weekly and monthly review meetings help her review work and set goals for the weeks and month ahead.

STRATEGISING AND GOAL SETTING:
WEEKLY AND MONTHLY REVIEWS

> @TheKiranBedi: With every monthly review we do we get sharper in our performance. To serve Puducherry better and more.
>
> 6 December 2018

For Dr Kiran Bedi work is all about communicating, networking, reviewing and following up all that is going on in the administrative set-up in Puducherry. She has a weekly review meeting with the chief secretary where she discusses all the issues of the week with him and also keeps track of all the correspondence between the Government of India and the Government of Puducherry. The chief secretary also gives her a report of the pending files so the LG's office can track and retrieve those files which are overdue.

The monthly review meetings involve all secretaries and heads of departments. During the meeting they evaluate inter department's performance, identify issues that need to be urgently attended to, set targets for the month ahead and also discuss policy matters. As an aggregation of minds, the monthly review lends itself well to yielding practical administrative solutions.

Dr Bedi also encouraged the departments to get more tech savvy and use dash board reviews. Here is a blog she wrote about dash board reviews so the team understands better how to use this system.

> What is a Dash Board? And how does it enhance administrative efficiency. Let us understand this.
>
> As this usage places all essential information of administrative departments (without compromising security) for decision and policy makers. At no additional cost, reducing paper work.
>
> It enhances openness, speed and honesty in its public services. Hence most essential for any administration to imbibe it. Like computers, this too is now essential for efficient and coordinated administration.
>
> Dash Board is like information on the screen of a computer which one can see, for analysis use for results or objectives if met.
>
> Such as grievance redressal disposal, main causes and areas affected, arrears of revenue, which department is collecting how much, which area affected for to concentrate on,

expenditure spent on all schemes through which we can assess the performance of departments. And their impact.

Which being, Financial and Administrative.

It is hence just an analysis tool for understanding and promoting efficient administration and good governance by way of understanding information.

(already in use by some of our existing depts in Puducherry, but presently in an isolated way. Such as grievance redressal, civil supplies, health schemes and more.

Lt Gov office is already using it in its Monthly Secretaries meeting held at Rajnivas.

However, for Puducherry Administration as a whole to benefit, it needs integration amongst all key departments. (Without losing control over their own information.)

This collation and analysis efficiently replace time consuming paper work for all departments. And saves time by easy analysis.

It in no way takes away anyone's administrative powers or positions. All use of information remains with officials. It's goes back to policy files. And due process.

It increases the analysis and performance capability of every official in-charge, whoever it is.

Password is to be with leadership as decided by the secretary concerned.

> Once this is understood in the right perspective there shall be no doubt in its usage.
>
> In fact, this implements the Right to Information Act section 4, in letter and spirit, mandated by law to do.
>
> Which means giving people information by yourself without being asked for.
>
> For instance, file tracking can be part of the dash board.
>
> Officers of the departments can know where their office file is.

Being fearless is synonymous with Dr Bedi and she believes in taking people by surprise. Her surprise and incognito rounds have been a reflection of her kindness and concern to look into the safety of people of Puducherry.

CONFIRMING TRUTHS
SURPRISE/INCOGNITO VISITS

> @TheKiranBedi: Just back from a night round. Went pillion riding on a scooter camouflaged. Felt Pondicherry safe for women, even at night. Shall repeat.
>
> 19 August 2017

I recall the day when the news channels flashed that Dr Kiran Bedi had gone on an incognito round in Puducherry on a bike to check on women's safety. Everybody wondered why a governor had to step out on such a round, that too on a two-wheeler so late at night. But this is Dr Kiran Bedi's commitment to ensuring proper public administration and what better way to take a reality check than to make an incognito visit or a surprise visit.

"We always have traffic complaints and when madam goes on such surprise checks and incognito checks, we get to see the reality. This in turn has helped make policing more visible, made enforcement of traffic rules more stringent and in the case of sanitation issues, it has made people more conscious and careful about garbage disposal," says S. Karthigayan, ADC to LG who has been with Dr Bedi through all these rounds.

Whether she made a surprise visit to a police station, or got off from her car to see how many people were wearing helmets and caught them unawares or went on that midnight bike round with comptroller Asha Gupta, every visit has been a revelation for her and it has helped her understand what needs to be attended to immediately. When LG comes back from an incognito check on the traffic situation with videos of cops standing on the roadside smoking, signals camouflaged with advertisements and most people not wearing helmets, then the police department is immediately put on high alert and work happens because you never know when madam is going to be out on rounds again!

And who can forget the morning when she was taking a walk on the beach, found it dirty and immediately asked for gloves and began cleaning it up. In no time the swachchata workers and other volunteers joined her and the beach was cleaned up.

Such surprise/incognito visits and actions speak volumes about the team's commitment towards providing a good public administration.

AN EXCERPT FROM HER BLOG ON THE MIDNIGHT INCOGNITO ROUND

SURAKSHA TO SWACHCHATA

From a midnight incognito #suraksha round to the 6 a.m. weekend #Swachh round, found Puducherry reasonably safe at night. But will be improved.

Also urge people to connect with PCT, 100 and inform their concerns. The night check was done incognito as a pillion rider on a two wheeler to personally check on how secure it was for women at night to be on the road or in a public place The round indicated the need to ensure police presence with mobility as a strong measure of crime prevention and response (being implemented from today).

Here is the assessment of the night round in disguise:

It seemed safe. But there was not a cop anywhere spotted. Also noisy bikers without silencers, triple riders who were over-speeding. We must have a motorcycle patrol and also a few cycle cops. At least from 11 p.m. to 4 a.m. daily. Taking a few rounds inside the bus stand, position outside railway station when the last train comes and just do rounds of the town. Also be outside the cinema hall after the last show.

Please implement this forth with (DGP + SSP). We must also have a night officer declared by written order who responds to an important night call and the PCR should know who it is. Shall be checking this time to time.

EXCERPT OF BLOG ON SURPRISE VISIT TO POLICE CONTROL ROOM

This morning paid a surprise visit to the police control room to review how were calls being recorded, particularly 1031 toll free which on request of complainant can be kept strictly confidential. Visit revealed that there was scope to improve inter-departmental coordination as well as internal communication. All such grievances must reach the beat staff through their daily morning roll calls taken by SHOs. Additional secretary Mr Srinivas will ensure henceforth all complaints recorded on 1031 toll free number are responded within 24 hours and also fed into our grievances portal to keep a track. Excessive staff deployed also needs some re-budgeting or fresh assessment to save and correctly deploy. Unclean premises also need to be cleaned up. Request all departments to ensure complaints received directly into their control rooms or through other sources are also carefully logged in andattended to.

These are those which are not logged into our computer system being monitored by Rajnivas desk of additional secretary. This group of grievances shall be checked by surprise anytime, any day by team Rajnivas.

MANAGEMENT LESSON

Mentoring is perhaps the most powerful method by which a leader can shape the future of her team members.

The various aspects of mentoring are:

M-model, E- empathise, N- nurture, T- teach, O-organise,

R-respond, I- inspire, N- network, G – goal set

As a leader, make the time and effort to get to know people on your team better, use your experience and skills to mentor them and guide them to see them perform better.

Be it meetings, visits or reviews, the strong underlying principle which drives all of these is the power of communication and the use of technology.

ENGAGING AND ENLIGHTENING:
THE USE OF COMMUNICATION AND TECHNOLOGY

Presented to Honble President & Union Home Minister published by Creative Team of RajNivas at the Annual Governor's, Lt Gov Conference at Rashtrapati Bhavan today. @rashtrapatibhvn @PMOIndia @HMOIndia @AshwaniKumar_92 @PIB_India @ANI These publications r on RajNivas website.

26 February 2019

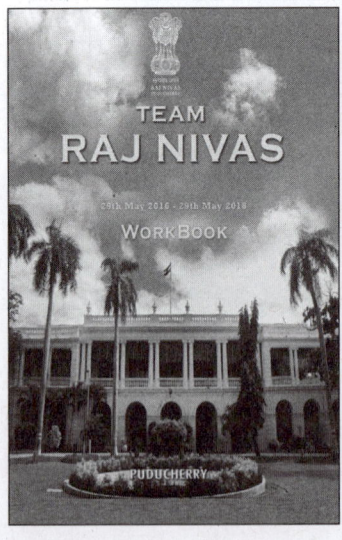

THE RAJNIVAS FOURTH ESTATE:
THE CREATIVE TEAM AND DOCUMENTATION

> @TheKiranBedi: Presented to Honble President & Union Home Minister published by Creative Team of RajNivas at the Annual Governor's,Lt Gov Conference at Rashtrapati Bhavan today. @rashtrapatibhvn@PMOIndia@HMOIndia@AshwaniKumar_92@PIB_India@ANI These publications r on RajNivas website..

When the leader believes in both the power of communication and making the best use of available technology, then the presence of a strong media team in her office is inevitable. The creative team is a core group of Team Rajnivas which handles timely dissemination of information across various communication platforms, be it social media, print media, broadcast media or via the dynamic Rajnivas website.

The social media handles of Rajnivas under the name Lgov_ Puducherry and the personal handles of Dr Kiran Bedi, both have a very significant and pervasive presence across various platforms. Dr Bedi's Linkedin account has been ranked as one of the top 25 accounts in the country.

The team not just engages with people through social media handles and WhatsApp groups, but is also instrumental in documenting all the work done at Rajnivas through various publications, making short films, videos and maintain an archive of photographs which are all a very valuable record for the office of the LG.

Dr Bedi is personally active on her twitter handle @TheKiranBedi and tweets about all issues of significance and she also communicates the same to the many WhatsApp groups she is a part of.Shealso leads and guides the creative team in all its endeavours.

Walk to Dr Bedi's residence office and you will be amazed at how meticulously she maintains all her documents. She believes that effective documentation is an integral aspect and building block of any organisation. Dr Bedi herself has guided the team on how to maintain the documents and these include both personal and official documents, photos, videos, print media clippings, etc. The system she has evolved makes data retrieval easy and it basically means to index all documents using key words which are hyper linked to the documents. The documents are used to retrieve details of various activities, for retaining as evidence or for reaching out to citizens. These repositories of data are also source-points for policies and rules as well as preserving the information for posterity.

To keep the communication channels simple and effective, Dr Bedi makes maximum use of WhatsApp and shares information through the various groups she is a part of.

CONNECTIVITY WITH A PURPOSE:
PROSPEROUS PUDUCHERRY WHATSAPP GROUP

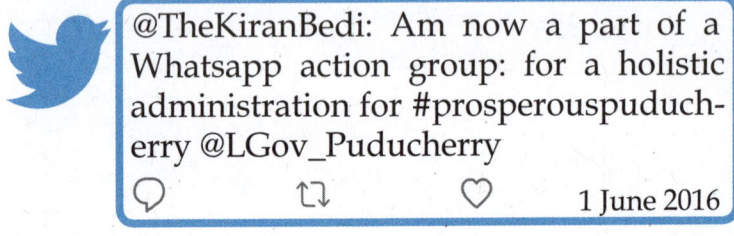

@TheKiranBedi: Am now a part of a Whatsapp action group: for a holistic administration for #prosperouspuducherry @LGov_Puducherry

1 June 2016

One of the first initiatives taken by Dr Kiran Bedi within days of taking over as LG was to form a WhatsApp group called the Prosperous Puducherry Group. When she took oath, she said she was here on a mission to make Puducherry a Prosperous Puducherry and this group, which consistsof officers to all departments and works towards ensuring instant responses to public grievances, was rightly christened the Prosperous Puducherry WhatsApp group.

"This group has been created for better coordination among officials and quick resolution of any civic issue. This system is much useful for immediate communication and to shorten the response time," says Theva Neethi Dhas OSD to LG.

The group comprises officers including Chief Secretary, the police chief, secretaries of several other departments, officials who deal with essential services to the public and police officers of different areas. The group has helped to promote coordination within the government and has facilitated sharing of valuable public information and issues which require immediate attention. This mode of communication cuts across hierarchies and unites the team with the purpose of serving the community. It has helped to increase the speed with which the government works and also helped create easy real time interface for the public.

TRANSPARENCY AT ITS BEST: DECLARATION OF WEEKLY DISPOSAL OF FILES

> @TheKiranBedi- RajNivas shares weekly whatever files it clears. This has stopped files from going missing. Also concerned now know where their matters are & cannot b misinformed. They too can demand copies of approvals. This transparency has empowered people & stopped rumours and misinformation
>
> ♡ 26 December 2017

As part of her efforts to bring in complete transparency in administration, in December 2017 Dr Kiran Bedi announced that the office of the Lieutenant Governor shall henceforth announce all important decisions taken by uploading a weekly bulletin of cleared files on the Rajnivas website.

In this weekly bulletin, Team Rajnivas declares details of every file it clears along with relevant decisions taken. The details disclosed in the bulletin include the date on which the file was received, the date on which it was cleared and the decision taken. This assures public of clarity and efficiency and also keeps people concerned with the files on the status of matters.

"The practice of declaring the list of files disposed during the week is very unique and forms part of the proactive disclosure mandated by the provisions of Right to Information Act, 2005. Usually in any government office the file passes through a long chain of going through various departments and through the hands of various elected representatives before any decision is taken. But here we make a voluntary disclosure of all files cleared and this list is uploaded every Saturday on our website. This practice is a very clear hallmark of our transparency," says Theva Neethi Dhas.

This list is also shared with the media and as much as it ensures transparency, it avoids any kind of unnecessary confusions. Underpinning each decision made at Rajnivas is justice, rule of law and financial prudence.

Approval of Hon'ble Lt. Governor was accorded in respect of the following subjects during the period from 04/08/2019 to 10/08/2019

Sl. No	LG Off. Receipt No. & Received Date	Department	File Subject	Decision	Despatched Date
1	182 / 22-07-2019	Home	Recommendation of Advisory Board regarding detention of Thiru Sundar @ Sakthivel S/o Muthukrishnan, Maduvupet, Puducherry under the provision of PPASA Act2008.	Accepted	06-08-2019
2	188 / 29-07-2019	Home	Recommendation of Advisory Board regarding detention of Thiru Sasi @ Sasikumar, S/o Iyyanar, Periyapet, Thirubuvanai, Puducherry under the provisions of PPASA Act, 2008.	Accepted	06-08-2019
3	198 / 02-08-2019	Finance	Release of Contingency fund towards settlement of rent payment as per court orders by Dte. of School Education	Approved	05-08-2019
4	200 / 02-08-2019	Chief Vigilance Office	Reference to MHA regarding initiation of RDA against Tvl. SCB Mohan, E.E (Retd), PWD and others based on the recommendations of the CBI, ACB, Chennai in RC 22(A)/2008.	Approved	06-08-2019
5	201 / 02-08-2019	Chief Vigilance Office	Initiating disciplinary proceedings against Thiru D.Rajendiran, JTP, Town and Country Planning, Karaikal who was chargesheeted by the CBI-ACB, Chennai in RC 13(A)/2007.	Approved	05-08-2019
6	202 / 02-08-2019	Chief Vigilance Office	Disciplinary proceeding against Thiru K.Alexander, Vice-Principal, School Education Department	Approved	05-08-2019
7	203 / 04-08-2019	Women & Child Dev.	Expr. sanction for disbursement of Old Age and Destitute Pensions for Rs.29,65,21,500/- to 1,54,847 nos. of beneficiaries for the month of July 2019 payable in August 2019.	Accorded	05-08-2019
8	204 / 05-08-2019	DP&AR	Continuance of 7 temporary posts for the period from 31.07.19 to 30.07.2020 in respect of LG Secretariat/Office of Council of Ministers, Puducherry.	Approved	05-08-2019
9	205 / 05-08-2019	Law	Enhancement of Counsellors fees in the Family Court, Puducherry.	Approved	05-08-2019
10	206 / 05-08-2019	DP&AR	Relieving on Transfer of 3 IAS Officers, namely Tvl. Tarsem Kumar, P. Jawahar & P. Parthiban.	Approved	05-08-2019

Approval of Hon'ble Lt. Governor was accorded in respect of the following subjects during the period from 04/08/2019 to 10/08/2019

Sl. No	LG Off. Receipt No. & Received Date	Department	File Subject	Decision	Despatched Date
11	207 / 06-08-2019	Information Technology	Deputation of Thiru R.Ilango, DPA as Computer Programmer to JIPMER.	Approved	06-08-2019
12	208 / 06-08-2019	Hr. & Tech. Education	Acceptance of resignation tendered by Dr.Shruti Joshi, Asst. Professor in Politics, Arignar Anna Govt. Arts & Science College, Karaikal.	Approved	06-08-2019
13	209 / 08-08-2019	Labour	Entrusting of Current duty charges for the posts of Principal in Govt. ITIs, Labour Department, Puducherry.	Approved	10-08-2019
14	210 / 08-08-2019	Chief Sectt. (CCD)	Appointment of Shri. M.R. Sampath Kumar, J.E., PWD as Personal Assistant to Chief Minister on deputation	Approved	10-08-2019
15	211 / 08-08-2019	DP&AR	Consideration of Thiru P. Deivanayagam, Asssistant (Retd) Electricity Dept., for promotion to the post of Superintendent on adhoc and notional basis.	Approved	10-08-2019
16	212 / 08-08-2019	Finance	Note of Voluntary Retirement from Service given by Thiru K.V.Ramakrishnan, JAO, DRDA, Puducherry.	Approved	10-08-2019
17	213 / 08-08-2019	DP&AR	Promotion of five (5) UDCs to the post of Assistant on notional basis on par with their juniors.	Approved	10-08-2019
18	214 / 08-08-2019	Commercial Taxes	Issue of rate notification under the Goods and Services Tax Act, 2017.	Approved	10-08-2019

// By Order //

(G. THEVA NEETHI DHAS)
Officer on Special Duty to Lt. Governor

The best way to reach out to the common man is through a monthly message which conveys to them all the work that the LG's secretariat is doing and also to appeal to them for community participation.

CONNECTING WITH COMMON MAN: MONTHLY MESSAGE TO CITIZENS

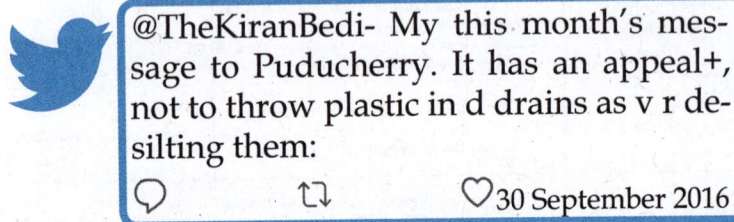

@TheKiranBedi- My this month's message to Puducherry. It has an appeal+, not to throw plastic in d drains as v r desilting them:

30 September 2016

If all across the nation citizens are listening to the honourable PM's Mann Ki Baat, then citizens of Puducherry listen to their LG through her monthly message "Valamikka Puducherry" broadcast by Doordarshan Puducherry as well as by All India Radio Puducherryy in its prime channel as well as in the Rainbow FM channel and also on Karaikal All India Radio.

Every month in the message, issues of priority and concern are brought up and citizens are kept apprised of the plans for the month ahead, given an account of the tasks the government has accomplished, the challenges it has overcome, appeals are made for community participation and residents are alerted about important developments.

While Dr Kiran Bedi delivers this message in English, her OSD gives a voice translation in Tamil, so the reach of the monthly message is far-and-wide.

These messages have certainly been impactful in reaching out to the public and involving them with the government towards making Puducherry a Prosperous Puducherry.

EXCERPT FROM MONTHLY MESSAGE AUGUST 2019

Vanakkam! This morning I am going to tell you a story of Team Rajnivas doing its 225th weekend morning round to Thondamanatham community centre. When we went to the community centre at Thondamanatham we found the gate broken, the premises full of garbage and unclean completely. Also, no water, toilets blocked and there was hardly anything right with that community centre of that village. Instead of telling them let's get it cleaned up and let's get it repaired, all of us present decided collectively that there is no tomorrow. We will clean it up right away. When a particular farmer of that village saw us cleaning, he on his own brought his tractor. His tractor started to work all along the periphery of the walls of the community centre and started to clean it up. Nobody told him, he started doing this by himself. Within an hour-and-a-half, all the community centre premises were clean.

Then the community decided to celebrate it the following day which was a Sunday by playing volleyball. We again went back on Sunday, the volley ball and the poles had been brought by the same people, the same residents of the same village. They put it up and women played hand ball and children played volley ball and throwball. Teams were formed and the Sub-Collector Saurav Shaswat gave away prizes to those women and youth who played. The Commune Commissioner Arumugam of Villianur shook hands with all the players. Team Rajnivas presented caps to all of them as participation. Team Rajnivas had also taken 60 plants to plant and all of us, NSS volunteers, the women and the children, we all worked together to plant the 60 trees all along the peripheral wall. The Director Rural Mr Ravi Prakash presented the keys of the community centre to the panchayat level federation. Friends, now it is the women who are managing the community centre and the gate has been repaired. No anti-social elements can now enter the premises and spoil the ground. This is an example when we all work together and don't wait for others. In every village, women should take up such initiatives and clean up their own community centres and make a Prosperous Puducherry.

> **MANAGEMENT LESSON**
> Communication is the core of leadership and a good leader makes every effort to communicate with people at all levels.
>
> As a leader for effective management you must communicate relentlessly, simplify your messages and be direct, listen to suggestions and encourage inputs from all, illustrate your communication through stories and affirm what you communicate through your actions.

When a leader communicates so effectively then networking and collaborating comes to her naturally, enabling her to start an outreach programme to help the community.

NETWORKING AND COLLABORATIONS

> **LEADERSHIP NUGGET**
> What you do want is people who can collaborate, listen, and build strong networks. The good news is you already have these people in your organization. Don't let them get drowned out.
> —@HarvardBiz @ForbesLeaders

GIVING BACK TO THE COMMUNITY
THE RAJNIVAS OUTREACH PROGRAM

> @TheKiranBedi-#TeamRajnivas as providers taking full support from CSR. Making #PuducherryResourceRich. "Raj Nivas Outreach" is "Abundance of Grace". RajNivas works together as one family to be need-providers led by @ashapdy @AshwaniKumar_92@ANI
>
> 5 March 2019

Someone once rightly said, "Without a sense of caring there can be no sense of community," and true to this saying Dr Bedi has always involved the community in her work. If she managed to reform Tihar with a zero government budget, it was purely through the community involvement and now as LG also she decided to bring in the community to be part of the Rajnivas Outreach Programmes.

"Rajnivas also reached out to needs outside the Rajnivas – coining the term Rajnivas Social Responsibility on the lines of CSR. Villages, water bodies, rural schools, public awareness causes, prison inmates reformation and health and hygiene programmes tapped social capital and CSR to create synergy of resources. Rajnivas has been a Peoples' Nivas which not only welcomed citizens into its precincts but also crossed over to public domain to actualise programmes," says Asha Gupta, who has been steering these outreach programmes under the guidance and mentorship of Dr Kiran Bedi.

One of the main programmes conducted under this outreach program has been the inmate reformation programme at the Kalapet Central Prison. The focus has been on crime prevention by reintegrating them by providing skill training conducted by NGOs. A brand called "Restore" has been created in collaboration with prison authorities to create sustainable livelihoods for inmates.

Another significant initiative of the Rajnivas Outreach Programme has been the adoption of TN Palayam village with a vision to empower villagers to become self-reliant. Since this village was adopted in December 2016, Rajnivas has worked with them in the field of education, health, eco corners and much more, helping this village evolve into a model of self-sustainability.

Apart from these initiatives, Rajnivas regularly collaborates with various groups to conduct book donation drives, bring in computers for government schools, conduct personality development and gender sensitisation workshops and even conduct nature treks for them.

"We have so many groups which come as visitors and most of them as admirers of our honourable LG madam. As she interacts with them, she notices their potential to collaborate with us and immediately encourages them to do so. And soon they come back to pool in resources with which they can help us. This is how the Rajnivas outreach programme has grown and continues to grow. It is the people's confidence is us that allows us to facilitate CSR and community involvement to bring about local transformation," says Asha Gupta.

A remarkable model of a CSR success story is how it helped to make Puducherry water rich. When Dr Bedi visited the water channels and saw that they needed to be desilted, that too using JCB machinery and also learnt that the PWD departments had no funds for the same, she immediately decided to bring in CSR collaborations from companies and educational institutions. She reached out through her personal twitter handle and requested for CSR support. Once the first donor came in, it gave her the confidence to look for more. Soon unprecedented support poured in, helping her raise over a crore of rupees to desilt both urban and rural water channels.

A young child Harini, who danced at the Rajnivas Pongal celebrations, received ₹1 Lakh from a philanthropist who watched her perform and was impressed with her talent. A post office account was opened in her name and she will receive this amount when she goes to college. She is now a part of the Rajnivas fraternity and this association will take her places.

People deem it an honour to associate with Dr Kiran Bedi and she too reciprocates by expressing her whole-hearted gratitude in the form of certificates and awards, which become a proud part of the profiles of people and companies who collaborate with Rajnivas. From pencils to desilting, the Rajnivas outreach programme is a remarkable model of collaboration that is worthy of being emulated by other states in the country.

Coopting leaders has been the underlying principal of Dr Bedi's leadership and she has been able to bring together various groups of leaders, including women from Puducherry administration, to make them solution providers.

TOWARDS COLLABORATION AND IMPROVEMENT: CO OPTING HUMAN RESOURCES

 @TheKiranBedi- A meeting of Women officers from different departments of Puducherry A meeting to create sisterhood in Puducherry Administration. Creating a culture of Self Help, Mutual Support, Collaboration not Competition. Shall meet every three months to celebrate.

19 March 2018

The durbar hall and the lawns of Rajnivas have become platforms for networking and interactions among public officials, NGOs, youth and senior citizens.

"One of the most significant meetings we had was with all women of Puducherry administration to help them bond together as sisters and evolve together. This group includes women across all hierarchies and has evolved. We have a WhatsApp group where we post about all activities especially about programs conducted on women's day at all offices," says Asha Gupta.

"We are meeting today to start our Sisterhood Of Women in Puducherry Administration, to stay connected through our WhatsApp group and meet once in three months. I want you to leave this meeting today as self-reliant leaders who are solution providers for all others," said Dr Kiran Bedi at the meeting she called to meet all women who work in Puducherry administration.

Training sessions have been conducted on dealing with domestic violence, digital transactions, rural development through commune commissioners and so on to encourage exchange of information and ideas among individuals and groups which have a common interest Rajnivas has organized 44 networking sessions with 6,186 citizens.

Empowering women has been a major focus of Team Rajnivas and not only has the team been able to help them overcome challenges like poverty but also been able to help them make the most of welfare schemes targeting women making them more self-reliant.

> **MANAGEMENT LESSON**
>
> Collaboration and networking strengthen your organisation. As a leader, build collaborations based on the human element and use it as a medium to bring a change in attitude and behaviour of the people in your organisation which also makes it an organizational change strategy. This helps in building trust and relationships amongst people you collaborate and network with.

Passionate and kind leadership is also all about rewarding performances and good work and Dr Bedi doesn't miss an opportunity to appreciate and applaud people around her.

APPRECIATION WITH KINDNESS: AWARDS AND RECOGNITION

@The Kiran Bedi- To encourage +recognise+ promote community leadership in areas of Water, Sanitation & Green Cover, RajNivas hereafter shall celebrate all its festivals by according #swachhatahisevaAwards. First such will b, this Diwali Eve for ALL CSR donors who r desilting 86 KM of Water Canals

7 October 2018

Team Rajnivas under the guidance of Dr Kiran Bedi believes in recognising outstanding work and services rendered by both government officials and individuals on a regular basis. NGOs and other groups which collaborate with Rajnivas for projects are always awarded certificates of recognition by the lieutenant governor. Apart from this Team Rajnivas instituted the Swachchata Hi Seva awards to honour all those who had supported the project Water Rich Puducherry. An award function was organised one evening at Rajnivas when these awards were given away to all the donors who helped in desilting water channels through their CSR.

The Front Runner awards were given to officers from various departments who went the extra mile to be with Team Rajnivas in all its initiatives. Some NGOs who have worked with Team Rajnivas in executing some of its outreach programmes were also awarded the Front Runner Awards.

To keep municipality officers and traffic encouraged, Dr Kiran Bedi meets them every Friday and rewards them for their weekly performance.

"We give weekly awards tomunicipality officers who effectively spot-fine shop keepers who throw garbage into drains because they do not keep dustbins and to Traffic Police officers and others who spot-fine road users for offences they commit under the Motor Vehicle Act," says Dr Kiran Bedi, who believes that these awards will keep them motivated to perform better.

Now working on Mission Green Puducherry, Rajnivas has also started recognising Green Ambassadors of Puducherry who have been leading tree planting movements for a long time.

The gifts comprise tokens of appreciation that have been received as gifts at Rajnivas and certificates.

MANAGEMENT LESSON

As a leader, people who work for you and with you look for appreciation and rewards because this encourages them. To make people feel important, it is the foundation of good leadership.

- Put praise in writing by regularly giving appreciation letters and certificates.
- Appreciate the smallest of achievements by giving rewards.
- Remember to reward all those who trust and go the extra mile to support your work.

A TRIP THAT WAS A TRUE REVELATION

 @thekiranbedi- #TeamRajnivas in Yanam. High Points: Visit to the Tidal lock options for flood prevention. Town Sanitation Issues: Demolition site of an old temple: Biomedical Waste disposal issues. An Island which Violated Envir Laws: Gifts to students: Open House which opened up d system

15 October 2019

When you are back from a trip that felt like an experience straight out of news on television then you are itching to write a few words about the memorable moments.

Yanam is a part of Puducherry. It is in Andhra Pradesh, close to Kakinada. Somewhere in a corner of my heart I was nurturing a wish to accompany Ma'am on her visit to Yanam. The wish did come true. A group of us went a day earlier to look around and assess the ground realities.

A quaint little town Yanam is spread over roughly 30 square km with a population of just

32,000 people. As we went around, we realised that this little town was plagued with many issues due to the rampant corruption from the politicians.

From garbage to sand mining, waste segregation to environment and even an issue related to a temple, each one of these was preventing the town from progressing. A beautiful little town with immense potential for tourism and development was victim of corruption and lack of proper governance.

As HLG Dr Kiran Bedi arrived and we accompanied her on a visit to all the places, the experience of driving with her in her cavalcade, watching people standing on either side of the road carrying black flags, black balloons and placards protesting against her (all driven by a local politician), jumping out of the car at every pit stop to listen to what the people were telling Ma'am, sprinting back into the car and many times hearing people screaming, "Kiran Bedi Zindabad", "Kiran Bedi ki jai", was an experience that gave me goose bumps. Being from the media, I am usually observing from the other side, but being part of the LG's team was a totally different experience. The security arrangements were impeccable and, thankfully, despite opposition and threats, the law-and-order situation was normal.

We had a long open house which was continued to the next day since we had as many as a hundred petitions. As HLG Ma'am said, we had released the bottled-up problems of the people of

Yanam, and now it was time for the administrator, the officers and the local police to act and bring about a change.

From instructing the regional administrator and the police to have regular open houses, to stressing on the importance of field visits to officers, the HLG spent every moment mentoring and guiding the team in Yanam.

HIGHLIGHTS OF THE TRIP

Visit to the site of flooding which revealed the need for fixing a gate below the culvert immediately, to prevent flooding in the next monsoon.

Solid waste management needs to be urgently attended to. The Kanak alpet dump yard also needed urgent attention as it was the breeding ground for many diseases.

Following complaints on biomedical waste disposal. The GH hospital needed to use proper waste segregation methods and different coloured bins.

Island number E5 had issues of violations of environmental laws and about ₹ 5 crores has been lost in the process.

Regarding the temple issue, the enquiry by HRI Commissioner revealed that temple accounts had not been audited for decades. The trustees would have to explain financial lapses. Also it was requested that they scientifically analysed the real age of the temple.

Open House was conducted in the evening and over a hundred petitions were received. As these could not be attended in one evening, the open house was carried over to 8 a.m. the next morning. Even then there was a long line of petitioners waiting. HLG moved out of the office and addressed a public meeting of the petitioners.

HLG also addressed the officers and stressed on the need for them to be visible, accessible to people, to do shramdaan and work towards a cleaner Yanam. She told them that the open house was an exercise for them to realise the power they have to serve. "You are afraid for your position. Instead, be fearless and serve. As officers be gentle and effective," said Dr Kiran Bedi as she mentored the officers to work as a team along with the regional administrator towards the betterment of Yanam.

MEDIA

Even before HLG Dr Bedi arrived at Yanam, there were numerous media reports floating around. The minister had said, "If Dr Bedi came to Yanam she would be taught a lesson." The media reports had also revealed that he threatened to have protests against HLG. Despite all this opposition, the team from Rajnivas made the visit. Media representatives were hovering around all the time, trying to capture special moments of the visit. HLG also addressed a press meet at the end of the trip and she was asked questions on issues which had not even been brought to her attention earlier or sent to Rajnivas. She was asked why she had not informed the minister about her visit when she had, in fact, invited him. There was a huge number of lies being traded by the media regarding the visit and at the same time information was being suppressed by them. They could have well played the role of being informers so the public would know the right situation and facts rather than being misguided by false media reports.

As we drove out of Yanam amid tight police protection, I could still hear people shouting Kiran Bedi ki jai! It is K for Kiran and K for kindness and Dr Bedi left a trail of her kindness in Yanam, giving the people hope that they wouldbe served well and also telling them to work with the administration towards making Yanam a new clean, green Yanam or a Kottha Yanam, as they are looking forward to calling it.

A PERFECT MODEL OF LEADERSHIP AND GOVERNANCE

> **LEADERSHIP NUGGET**
>
> Paradigms are powerful because they create the lens through which we see the world . ...if you want small changes in your life, work on your attitude. But if you want big and primary changes work on your paradigm.
>
> —Stephen Covey

True to the above, the Rajnivas model of best practices which evolved under the leadership of Dr Kiran Bedi has worked on paradigm shifts and helped bring in significant changes in the administration of Puducherry. The most effective techniques which can help any organisation perform better include:

Rather than breaking a silo encourage team work.

Have your vision and purpose of work clear and motivate your team to work with you towards achieving those goals.

Make yourself visible and accessible so people can hear from you directly rather than receive work emails and other communications.

Collaborate and work together in informal work groups.

Keep the public engaged as stake holders so they know they can reach out to you and work with you.

Fix a time of the day to go on field visits so you can identify your daily areas of work which require improvement.

Most importantly, keep yourself energised and motivated to be a problem-solver and work without fear or favour.

What has helped Dr Kiran Bedi be the administrator and leader she is has been purposeful kindness. A study at Harvard Business School by Amy Cuddy and her research partners says that even before establishing their own credibility or competence, leaders who project warmth are more effective than people who lead with toughness. Kindness helps to build trust. Studies reveal that the four best ways that help to practice purposeful kindness are kindness in recognising people; kindness in supporting people when they need guidance and help; kindness in caring for your team and understanding that they are also people, have families, have issues and empathising with them; and, most importantly, be kind while giving feedback rather than being overly critical.

Dr Kiran Bedi, not just as a lieutenant governor but also a person, is the best example of someone who practises purposeful kindness. She has led with kindness and it is her kindness which has helped the officials in Puducherry learn so much from her. The departments perform better, grievances have been addressed and people have a loving leader who doesn't speak the local language Tamil, but speaks kindness and is always ready to help them, and even give them an assuring hug.

The Dalai Lama said, "Be kind whenever possible, it is always possible." Dr Kiran Bedi follows this maxim and her work as LG stands testimony for this. Her leadership is the best example of Where Kindness Truly Spoke!

GRATITUDE

> Gratitude makes sense of our past, brings peace for today and creates a vision for tomorrow.
> — Melody Beattie

In writing this book I would like to express my gratitude to the following people without whose help and support this would not have been possible.

The Almighty for all his grace and blessings in giving me the strength and the vision to work on this book

My mother from whom I have acquired the genes for writing and who continuously pushes me to keep writing. My sister and her family for always encouraging me to pursue my talent in writing.

Dr Kiran Bedi, who has been a mother, a guide and mentor to me and completely encouraged me to write this book and guided me through every step of it

All the officers at Rajnivas – the 10 a.m. team – Shri Theva Neethi Dhas, OSD to the Lieutenant

Governor, Shri Sundaresan, Additional Secretary, Shri Sridharan, Private Secretary, Smt. Asha Gupta, Comptroller of Household, Dr Bascarane, Chief Grievance Officer, Shri Karthikayan, ADC and Shri Kumaran, PRO who steer the entire functioning of Rajnivas and most willingly spoke to me about all the activities at Rajnivas helping me structure the book.

The entire Creative Team at Rajnivas which I am a part of for helping me in all my work. Vijay and Poonguzhali the videographer team for sharing the leadership videos with me. Special thanks to my friend Beena Sivan who gave her valuable inputs whenever needed. The research team of Pooja Lal, Isha Arora and Tilak Ambalanathan for the support

A Manikanadan the photographer at Rajnivas for sharing all the pictures which I have used in this book.

My designers A.S. Diwakar and S. Riswan from Compuprint who worked so painstakingly in helping me put this book together.

My friend Sanjay Pinto who graciously accepted to write the foreword for the book

India Vision Foundation for all the support extended in bringing out this book.

I thank Sterling Publishers and Mr S K Ghai for having shown faith in my work.

I also wish to thank my editor Mr Sanjiv Sarin for meticulously editing my book.

ABOUT THE AUTHOR

Shivani Arora is a Chennai-based freelance journalist with almost 20 years of experience writing for national newspapers and magazines. She currently contributes to the *Times of India*. Shivani has conceptualised and authored six coffee-table books.

She is a linguistic expert and her work includes translation of several children's books from English to Hindi. Her forte is writing on health issues.

At present she is the social media editor for *Diwwaaas*, a diabetes awareness project for women.

Shivani is a history graduate from Stelle Maris. Her academic achievements include two post graduate degrees in public administration and Hindi literature and a post graduate diploma in translation. Her hobbies include reading, travelling and she loves meeting people.

Her association with Dr Kiran Bedi goes back to her teenage days when she started idolising her, although she first met her only in 2010 at a book-launch event. She continues to look up to Dr Bedi, who inspires at her every moment to grow, to evolve and to believe that its always possible to achieve every dream of hers.

Other Books by
KIRAN BEDI

As I See...
Kiran Bedi
978 81 207 8186 3   ₹ 300

**Empowering Women...
As I See**   *Kiran Bedi*
978 81 207 8114 6   ₹ 200

**Be The Change Fighting
Corruption**   *Kiran Bedi*
978 81 207 7716 3   ₹ 195

Issues & Views
Kiran Bedi
978 81 207 5068 5   ₹ 299

It's Always Possible *Kiran Bedi*
978 81 207 2886 8 ₹ 500

e-mail: mail@sterlingpublishers.in
visit: www.sterlingpublishers.in